Shortly after becoming a bis
Frances de Chantal, a wido
there grew a deep spiritual f
the spiritual director of Jan.
founded the religious order of nuns known ᴀₛ ₋
the Visitation, or the Visitandines. St. Francis de Sales was also for a time the confessor of Blessed Marie of the Incarnation (Madame Barbe Acarie), a wife, mother of six children, Parisian hostess, mystic, and foundress of five Carmelite convents.

St. Francis de Sales wrote two of the greatest Catholic masterpieces on the spiritual life: the *Introduction to the Devout Life* and *Treatise on the Love of God*. The former shows how holiness is possible for all people in the state of grace, including people living in the world. This book was a bestseller in the 17th century and is still popular today. The *Treatise on the Love of God* covers all aspects of the virtue of charity, the supernatural love of God. St. Francis de Sales' pamphlets against the Calvinist heresy have been gathered together into a book and given the title *Controversies*. The arguments presented in this book are just as unanswerable today as when they were written. Because of his writings, St. Francis de Sales has become the patron of writers and journalists; he has also been designated patron saint of the Catholic press.

St. Francis de Sales died at age 55, in the year 1622. His beatification, which occurred the very year he died, was the first formal beatification ever held in St. Peter's Basilica. He was canonized in 1665, and was declared a Doctor of the Universal Church by Pope Pius IX in 1877. With this declaration the Church presented the teachings of St. Francis de Sales to all the faithful as a sure guide to true Catholic doctrine and the ways of the spiritual life—a sure guide to Heaven.

PREFACE

It is a joy to welcome the English translation of the Sermons on Our Lady by Saint Francis de Sales. It is especially through his masterpiece, *Introduction to the Devout Life,* that the Doctor of the Church is known throughout the Christian world. The role of Our Lady as the Mother of God is not sufficiently appreciated. The publication of these thirteen Marian sermons will help all to see that Mary is an essential element of his spirituality.

It is especially as "model" of the devout life that Our Lady is depicted by Saint Francis de Sales. With his typical gentleness and contemplative spirit, the saint stresses several times in these sermons the basic beatitude of Our Lady: She hears the Word of God and keeps it. He exhorts us to do the same. To be more precise, it is Mary, the meek and humble Virgin, always obedient to the Word, whom this master of spirituality describes for our imitation. Because the Mother of God is the exemplar of the Christian life, the majority of these "Marian" sermons deal more with the Christian virtues than with Mary herself. His purpose, then, is not to compose a scholarly Mariological treatise. Rather, in his evangelically childlike manner, he preaches on the basic qualities of our life in Christ—especially humility—which so beautifully radiate through Mary. Although these sermons are for the most part directed to his Visitation Nuns, for whom Mary is the "Mother," the "Abbess," they are profitable for all Christians.

If one were to examine these sermons according to the

criteria stipulated by His Holiness, Pope Paul VI, in his Apostolic Exhortation *Marialis Cultus (On the Right Ordering of Devotion to Mary)*, their beauty becomes clearer. For although the sermons antedate the Apostolic Exhortation by approximately three and a half centuries, these works fulfill the requirements of Paul VI for solid devotion to the Mother of God.

The first two guidelines given to us by *Marialis Cultus* can be summarized by declaring that the ultimate source of all devotion to Mary must be Scripture as lived, prayed and taught by Holy Mother Church. Nothing characterizes these sermons more than their scriptural and liturgical foundations. Fidelity to the Word of God as preached by the Catholic Church is the very spirit of this Bishop of Geneva who tended his flock during the upheavals of the post-reformation era. He therefore constantly quotes Scripture, betraying his predilection for a mystical interpretation of the *Song of Songs*. The teachings of the Church are his constant guide.

Saint Francis de Sales' allegorical, mystical use of Scripture—typical of many of the Fathers of the Church—seems foreign to contemporary scientific studies. Also, the teachings of the Church concerning Mary, Mother of God and Mother of the Church, have been further developed and clarified during the centuries since these sermons were delivered. However, one is not to search for modern scriptural interpretations or a contemporary Mariology in these conferences which date from the early part of the seventeenth century. It is their solid, contemplative insight into Mary as model of Christian life which has lasting value.

The second pair of guidelines given to us by Paul VI is especially important in understanding the thought of Saint Francis de Sales. *Marialis Cultus* calls for a Mariology which is ecumenical and anthropological: ecumenical in the sense that the truth must be proclaimed in a way that will attract, and not unnecessarily offend, our separated brethren: anthropological in the sense that the preaching must be in accord with the culture and needs of the people addressed—always, however, remaining within the ambit of the Catholic Faith.

Some may deny that these Marian sermons are ecumenical. There are expressions (e.g., the divine Mary), opinions (e.g., endowed with the use of reason from the first moment of her conception, Mary is from the beginning of her existence a true contemplative), which some contemporary scholars would classify as offensive to many non-Catholics and Catholics alike. However, it must never be forgotten when reading these sermons that this mild-mannered seventeenth-century Bishop of Geneva is boldly preaching in the language of *his* age, expressing the opinions of *his* time. How could it be otherwise? Saints too are children of their times.

Moreover, Saint Francis de Sales attracted untold numbers to the Church by observing the primary rule of ecumenical dialogue: Never dilute the truths of the Faith in order to achieve a facade of unity. Although he espouses opinions of his time which some today would term "extravagant," he does differentiate between what is necessary for the profession of the Catholic faith and what is not. These sermons are intended not for a theological convocation nor for an ecumenical gathering, but primarily for the contemplative Order he founded with Saint Jane Frances de Chantal, the Visitation Nuns.

These sermons admirably fulfill, therefore, the criterion of "anthropological": Their expressions and style mesh with the culture of the times, they speak to the mindset of the audience, they address the needs of his people, primarily his Visitation Nuns. To expect to find in these works the concise style of contemporary preaching, the insights of modern theological studies, is not only unrealistic but does no honor to this Bishop of Geneva who had the difficult task of proclaiming the Gospel amidst the turmoil of the early 1600's. That the sermons of this Doctor of the Church spoke powerfully to the hearts of his people is beyond doubt, since so many lapsed Catholics returned to the faith because of his preaching.

What proves the importance of these sermons is the fact that they are, as *Marialis Cultus* demands of all Marian devotion, centered on Christ, the Incarnate Second Person of the Trinity, the Head of His Body, the Church. These works of Saint Francis de Sales are distinctly Christocentric. Mary, explains this Doctor of the Church, receives all her gifts from the Father through the Son so that she may praise God and be a living example of total surrender to Christ Jesus. Mary is never taken out of this necessary Christological context. She is the model who leads all of us to a deeper life in Christ. Nothing demonstrates this thought of Francis de Sales better than the final words of his sermon on the Immaculate Conception: " . . . if you ask her: 'Mother, what do you wish us to do for you?' no doubt she will answer that she desires and wishes that you do what she asked to be done at the celebrated marriage feast of Cana in Galilee when the wine gave out. She said to those who came to tell her of their need: *Do whatever* my Son *tells you.* If then you listen faithfully, you will hear in your heart those very words addressed to you: *Do whatever* my Son *tells you.* May God give us the grace to listen to her in this life and in the other. Amen."

Surely a debt of gratitude is owed to the Visitation Nuns for making these Marian sermons available to the English-speaking world. The quiet contemplative soul will readily experience their beauty. All readers will be led by their peaceful pace and depth of personal insight to a more intense union with the Lord.

✠ John Joseph Cardinal Carberry
Archbishop Emeritus of Saint Louis
May 31, 1985
Feast of the Visitation

TRANSLATOR'S NOTE

The thirteen sermons on Our Lady contained in this book were translated from St. Francis de Sales' *Oeuvres,* vols. VII, IX, and X (Annecy: Niérat, 1892-1964).

The first volume of this series, *Sermons of St. Francis de Sales on Prayer,* includes an Introduction on the Origins and Value of the Sermons which was also taken from the Annecy edition.

The ancient image of *Notre Dame de Bonne Délivrance*—"Our Lady of Kind Deliverance," the Black Virgin, through whose intercession St. Francis de Sales was delivered from terrible agony of soul at age 19.

THE ASSUMPTION
OF THE BLESSED VIRGIN MARY

*Sermon for the Feast of the Assumption, August
15, 1602, concerning Our Lady's life on earth
after Our Lord's Ascension, Our Lady's death, the
close union between Mary and her Son during His
Passion, the voluntariness of Our Lord's death,
the cause of Mary's death, Our Lady's exemption
from the law of corruption, the "perfumes" of
graces and virtues which she brought with her to
Heaven, the honor due to Mary, God as the
source of all Mary's graces, the true way to honor
Our Lady, and the true Christian teaching on the
mediation of Our Lady and the saints.*

*"Who is this coming up from the desert,
flowing with delights, leaning upon her
Lover?"—Song 8:5*

The Ark of the Covenant had been kept under tents and
pavilions for a long time when at length the great King
Solomon placed it in the rich and magnificent Temple
which he had prepared for it. [*1 Kgs.* 8]. The rejoicings in
Jerusalem were so great at this time that the blood of the
sacrifices flowed in the streets, the air was thick with
clouds from so much incense and perfume, and the homes
and public places resounded with the canticles and psalms
sung by all with music and melodious instruments.

But, O God,[1] if the reception of that ancient Ark was so

1

solemn, what must we not think to have been that of the
new Ark? I speak of the most glorious Virgin Mother of
the Son of God on the day of her Assumption. O joy incomprehensible! O feast full of marvels which makes
devout souls, the true daughters of Zion, cry out in admiration: "Who is this coming up from the desert?" And indeed
these facts are admirable: The Mother of Life is dead;
death is resurrected and ascends to the abode of life. What
a feast of consolation! She has ascended for the honor of
her Son and to arouse in us a great devotion. This is the
subject of which I will treat with you, O my people, but I
cannot do so well unless I first obtain the assistance of the
Holy Spirit. *Ave Maria.*

In the beginning God placed in the heavens two lights.
The one, because of its great brilliance, was called the
greater light; the other was named the lesser—the greater
one to enlighten and govern the day, the lesser to enlighten
and govern the night. [*Gen.* 1:16]. For, though our Creator
willed that there should be changes of day and night, and
that the shades of night should succeed the brightness of
day, being Light Himself [*Jn.* 1:5] He did not will that
darkness and night should remain completely devoid of
light. Having created the greater light to govern the day,
He created a lesser light to govern the night so that the
obscurity of the night's darkness might be tempered by
means of its brightness.

This same God, with His holy Providence, determining
to create the spiritual world of His Church, placed over it
as in a divine vault of Heaven two great lights: one greater,
the other lesser. The greater is His Son Jesus Christ our
Saviour and Master, abyss of light, source of splendor, true
Sun of justice. [*Heb.* 1:3; *Mal.* 3:20]. The lesser is the most
holy Mother of this great Son, all-glorious Mother, all
resplendent and truly more beautiful than the moon. [*Song*
6:10].

Now, this greater Light came here upon earth. The Son
of God assumed our human nature. He is the true Sun

which comes over our hemisphere and makes the light and the day—happy day, so long desired, which lasted for about 33 years, during which He enlightened the land of the Church by the radiance of His miracles, example, teachings, and holy words! But at length when the hour came in which this precious Sun must set and take Its radiance to the other hemisphere of the Church, Heaven and the angelic hosts, what could be expected but the obscurity of a dark night? And the night came all too quickly after the day. What were so many afflictions and persecutions which came upon the Apostles but a night?

But this night had also its light which brightened it so that the darkness was more tolerable. For the Blessed Virgin remained on earth among the disciples and the faithful. We cannot doubt this, since St. Luke in the Acts testifies that Our Lady was with the disciples on Pentecost Day and that she persevered with them in prayer and communion. [*Acts* 2:1-4, 1:14]. Thus, they are convicted of error who say that she died with her Son because of the words of Simeon who foretold that a sword would pierce her soul through. [*Lk.* 2:35]. But I will soon expound on this passage and demonstrate by its true meaning that Our Lady did not die with her Son.

Let us first consider the reasons why her Son left her in this world after His own departure. (1) This light was needed for the consolation of the faithful who were in the night of afflictions. (2) Her remaining here below gave her an opportunity to achieve an accumulation of good works so great that it could be truly said of her: Many daughters have gathered together riches, but you have surpassed them all! [*Prov.* 31:29, *Douay*]. (3) As soon as Our Lord died and ascended to Heaven, some heretics were saying that He had not had a natural and human body but only an imaginary one. The Virgin, His Mother, in remaining after Him, served as a reliable witness of the truth of His human nature, thereby already beginning to verify what we sing of her: "You, O Holy Virgin, have destroyed all heresies throughout the world." Thus did she live after the death of her Life, that is to say, of her Son, and even long after His Ascension, though the number of the years is not definitely known. But they could not have been less than 15, which would have made her 63 when she died. At least 63, I say, inasmuch as others, and with more probability, would have her live until she was 72. But that matters little. It suffices for us to know that this holy Ark of the New Covenant remained in this desert of the world under tents and pavilions after the Ascension of her Son.

If this fact is certain, as it truly is, it is equally certain that at the end this Holy Lady died—not that the Scriptures explicitly say so, for I can find no word in the Scripture that says that the Virgin died. Ecclesiastical Tradition alone assures us of the fact, and so does Holy Church, which confirms this Tradition in the prayer she uses in the Mass of this feast. It is true that Scripture teaches us in general terms that all die, and that no human being is exempt from death. But it does not say that all are dead nor even that all those who have lived have already died. On the contrary, it exempts certain ones such as Elijah, who, without dying, was carried up to Heaven in a chariot of fire, and Enoch, who was taken away by Our Lord before he tasted death [*2 Kgs.* 2:11; *Gen.* 5:24; *Heb.* 11:5], and also St. John the Evangelist, the one I think to be most probable according to the word of God as I have demonstrated to you before on his feast in May. [*Jn.* 21:22]. These three saints are not dead. Yet they are not exempt from the law of death, because if they are not dead they will die at the end time under the persecution of Antichrist, as appears in Chapter 11 of the Book of Revelation. [*Rev.* 11:7].

Why may we not say the same of the Mother of God, namely, that she is not yet dead but will die at some future time? Certainly, if anyone wished to maintain this opinion we could not refute it by the Scripture, and according to your principles, O adversaries of the Catholic Church, it would be well-founded. But the truth is that she died and was buried, as well as her Son and Saviour. For though the fact cannot be proved by Scripture, yet Tradition and the Church, which are infallible witnesses, assure us of it.

Certain then that she died, let us now consider what kind of death she died. What death was so foolhardy as to dare to attack the Mother of Life, the Mother whose Son had conquered death and its sting, which is sin? [*1 Cor.* 15:55-56]. Be attentive, my dear listeners, for this point deserves consideration. I will soon have responded to the question, but it will not be easy for me to prove and explain it well.

My answer in a word is that Our Lady, Mother of God, died of the death of her Son. The fundamental reason is that Our Lady had only one same life with her Son and thus could have but only one same death with Him. She lived only by the life of her Son. How could she die of any other death but His? They were in truth two persons, Our Lord and Our Lady, but of one heart, one soul, one spirit, one life. For if the bond of charity so bound and united the Christians of the early Church that St. Luke assures us that they were of one heart and one mind [*Acts* 4:32], with how much greater reason may we not say and believe that the Son and the Mother, Our Lord and Our Lady, were only one soul and one life?

Consider the great Apostle St. Paul. He felt such a union and bond of charity between his Master and himself that he professed to have no other life but that of the Saviour: The life I live now is not my own; Christ is living in me. [*Gal.* 2:20]. O my people, this union, this fusion and bond of hearts which made St. Paul speak such words was great, but not to be compared with that between the Heart of the Son Jesus and that of the Mother Mary. For the love which Our Lady bore to her Son far surpassed that which St. Paul bore to his Master, inasmuch as the names of mother and son are more excellent in matters of affection than the names of master and servant. Hence, if St. Paul lived only of the life of Our Lord, Our Lady also lived only of the same life, but more perfectly, more excellently, more completely.

Now if she lived of His life, she also died of His death. And indeed the good old man Simeon had long before predicted this kind of death for Our Lady when, holding her Child in his arms, he said to her: And a sword will pierce your own soul. [*Lk.* 2:35, *Douay*]. Consider the words. He does not say: "A sword will pierce your body," but he says: "your soul." What soul? "Your own soul," said the prophet. The soul of Our Lady, then, is to be pierced, but by what sword, by what dagger? The prophet does not say. Nevertheless, since there is question of the soul and not of the body, of the spirit and not of the flesh, we must not understand a material and physical sword but a spiritual sword which can attack the soul and spirit. [*Heb.* 4:12].

Now I find three swords which can smite the soul. (1) The sword of the word of God, which, as the Apostle says, is sharper than any two-edged sword. [*Heb.* 4:12]. (2) The sword of sorrow which the Church understands from the words of Simeon: Your own soul, she says, was pierced by the sword of sorrow.

> Through her heart His sorrow sharing,
> All His bitter anguish bearing,
> Now at length the sword has passed.
> [*Stabat Mater*]

(3) The sword of love of which Our Lord speaks: It is not peace I have come to bring, but a sword [*Matt.* 10:34], which is the same as when He says: I have come to light a fire on the earth. [*Lk.* 12:49]. And in the Song of Songs, the Spouse² regards love as a sword by which He has been wounded, saying: You have wounded My Heart, My sister, My spouse. [*Song* 4:9, *Douay*]. The soul of Our Lady was pierced by these three swords in the death of her Son, and principally by the last, which includes the other two.

When we strike a great and powerful blow upon an ob-

ject, all that it touches receives a counter-blow. The body
of Our Lady was not joined to, nor did it touch, that of her
Son in the Passion. But as to her soul, it was inseparably
united to the soul, heart and body of her Son, so that the
blows which the blessed body of the Saviour received on
the Cross caused no wound to the body of Our Lady, but
they gave a mighty counter-blow to her soul, so that the
prophecy of Simeon was verified. Love is accustomed to
receive the counter-blows of the afflictions of the beloved.

Who is weak that I am not affected by it? Who is scan-
dalized that I am not aflame with indignation? Who
receives a blow of pain and I do not receive the counter-
blow? said the holy Apostle. [*2 Cor.* 11:29]. Yet the soul of
St. Paul did not touch the rest of the faithful so closely as
the soul of Our Lady touched and was firmly attached to
Our Lord. No union with His soul and with His body is
greater than hers, for she was His source, His root, His
Mother. It is no wonder, then, if I say that the sorrows of
the Son were the swords which pierced the soul of the
Mother.

Let us explain a little more clearly. An arrow aimed
straight at a person, having pierced his body, may also
wound those who are next to him and touching him. Our
Lady's soul was joined in perfect union to the Person of
her Son. Her soul was knit to her Son. Jonathan's soul
became closely bound to the soul of David, says the Scripture. [*1 Sam.* 18:1]. The soul of Jonathan was bound or
knit to that of David, so intimate was their friendship. Consequently, the thorns, the nails, the lance which pierced the
head, the hands, the feet, the side of Our Lord, passed
through them to pierce the soul of the Mother. Therefore I
may say in all truth, O holy Virgin, that your soul was
pierced with the love, with the sorrow, and with the words
of your Son.

As for love, oh how deeply it wounded you when you
saw a Son die whom you had so loved and adored. As for
His sorrow, how keenly did it touch you, mortally wound-

ing all your joy, your pleasure, and your consolation! As
for His words, so sweet yet so bitter, they were as so much
storm and wind to fan the fire of your love and your sorrows and to batter the boat of your heart, already almost
broken in the tempest of a sea of so much bitterness! Love
was the archer, for without it sorrow would not have had
sufficient movement to attack your soul. Sorrow was the
bow which shot the interior and exterior words, as so many
arrows that had no other target but your heart.

Alas, how was it possible that arrows so loving were so
painful? Let us not forget that the honeyed stingers of the
bees are extremely painful to those who are stung by them,
and it seems that the sweetness of the honey quickens the
sharpness of the point. Truly, O my people, the sweeter
were the words of Our Lord the more piercing they were to
the Virgin His Mother, and they will be so to us also if we
love her Son. What sweeter word than that which He spoke
to His Mother and St. John [*Jn.* 19:26-27], words that
were an undeniable witness to the constancy of His love,
His solicitude, His affection for this holy Lady. Nevertheless, without a doubt they were words that were extremely
painful for her. Nothing makes us feel more keenly the sorrow of a friend than the assurances he gives us of his love.

But if you please, let us return to our subject. It was at
that moment that Our Lady's soul was pierced by the
sword. And why, you say to me, did she not die at that moment? I have already said that some who maintain that she
did have erred gravely, and Scripture bears witness that she
was still living on the day of Pentecost and that she persevered with the Apostles in the exercise of prayer and
communion. Moreover, the tradition is that she lived for
many years after. But listen, does it not often happen that a
stag is wounded by the hunter, yet escapes with its shaft
and its wound and goes off to die many days after in a
place far distant from where it received the wound? Certainly Our Lady was struck and wounded by the dart of
pain in the Passion of her Son on Mount Calvary, yet she

did not die immediately but bore her wound for a long time, and from it she finally died. O loving wound! O wound of charity, which was so cherished and loved by the heart you wounded!

Aristotle and Pliny relate that the wild stags and goats of Crete have a cunning trick, or rather a wonderful instinct. When pierced by an arrow, they seek out the herb, Cretan dittany, which rejects and expels the arrow from the body. But who is the Christian who has not been wounded at some time by the dart of the Saviour's Passion? Where is the heart that has not been struck, considering his Saviour scourged, tortured, bound, nailed, crowned with thorns, crucified? I do not know if I dare to say it, but the greater part of Christians resemble the men of Crete, of whom the Apostle speaks: "Cretans have ever been liars, beasts and lazy gluttons!" [*Titus* 1:12]. At least I can say that many resemble the wild stags of Crete. Having been wounded and struck in their soul by the Saviour's Passion, they immediately have recourse to the dittany of worldly consolations, by which the darts of divine love are rejected and erased from their memory. In contrast the holy Virgin, feeling herself wounded, cherished and carefully guarded the shafts by which she had been pierced, and never desired to reject them. This was her glory, this was her triumph; and consequently, of this she desired to die—as at the end she did. So did she die of the death of her Son, though not at the same time.

Now, ought we not stay here? This subject is so pleasing in my opinion. Our Lady died of the death of her Son. But her Son—of what death did He die? Here are new fires to inflame our hearts, O Christians! Our Lord suffered infinitely in both soul and body. There are no sorrows in this world comparable to His. See the afflictions of His heart; see the Passion of His body; look, I beg you, and see: Is any suffering like His? [*Lam.* 1:12]. Nevertheless, all these sorrows, all these afflictions, all these blows of the hand, of the reed, the thorns, the scourging, the hammer, the lance could not make Him die. Death had not sufficient power to render itself victorious over such a life; it had no point of access. How then did He die?

O Christians, love is strong as death. [*Song* 8:6, *Douay*]. Love desired that death should enter into Our Lord, so that by His death, love could be spread abroad into all people. Death desired to enter there, but it could not do so of itself. It waited the hour, blessed hour for us, in which love gave it entrance and delivered over to it Our Lord, nailed hands and feet. What death was unable to do, love which is as strong as death undertook and accomplished. He died of love, this Saviour of my soul. Death could do nothing except by means of love: He was offered because it was His own will. [*Is.* 53:7, *Douay*].

It was by His own choice that He died and not by the power of evil. I lay down My life; no one takes it from Me, but I lay it down freely. [Cf. *Jn.* 10:17-18]. Any other man would have died from so many sufferings; but Our Lord, who holds in His hands the keys of death [*Rev.* 1:18] and of life, could have resisted forever the efforts of death and the effects of sufferings. But no, He did not will it so. The love He bore us, like another Delilah, took away all His strength [*Jgs.* 16:19], allowing Him to die willingly. This is why it is not said that His spirit went out from Him but that He gave it up. *Emisit Spiritum.* [*Mt.* 27:50; *Jn.* 19:30]. And St. Athanasius notes that He bowed His head before dying: *Inclinato capite, emisit spiritum* [*Mt.* 27:50; *Jn.* 19:30], to call death, which otherwise would not have dared to approach. This is also why He cried out in a loud voice while dying [*Mt.* 27:50; *Lk.* 23:46], to show that He had sufficient strength not to die, but that He willed it. It was the maxim He Himself had given: There is no greater charity than this: to lay down one's life for one's friends. [*Jn.* 15:13].

It was death from love then, and it is this that makes His sacrifice of the Cross a holocaust: because it was consumed by this invisible, but so much the more ardent fire of His

Divine Charity, which rendered Him—and not the Jews or the Gentiles who crucified Him—the sacrificer in this sacrifice, inasmuch as they could not have been able to bring death upon Him by their deeds if His love, by the most excellent act of charity which ever was, had not per- mitted and commanded the final effect. All the torments they inflicted upon Him would have remained ineffectual if He had not willed to allow them to take hold on His life and given them power over Himself. You would have no power over Me whatever unless it were given you from above. [*Jn.* 19:11].

Now, since it is certain that the Son died of love and that the Mother died of the death of the Son, we must not doubt that the Mother died of love. But how? You have observed that in seeing her Son die she was wounded by the wound of love on Mount Calvary. From that moment on she received such assaults from this love, she experienced so many transports, this wound became such a burning fire that in the end it was impossible that she should not die from it. She could only languish with love. Her life was no more than swoonings and ravishments from it. It was wast- ing away from so much passion, so that she could well say: Strengthen me with raisin cakes, refresh me with apples, for I am faint with love. [*Song* 2:5].

Amnon, captivated by the infamous love of Tamar, became so sick from it that they saw him waste away and die. [*2 Sam.* 13]. Oh, indeed, how much more active and powerful is Divine Love! Its object, its principle is so much greater. That is why there is nothing strange in my saying that Our Lady died from it. She always bore the wounds of her Son in her heart. For some time she suffered them without dying from them, but at the end she died from them without suffering. O passion of love, O love of the Passion!

Alas, her treasure, that is to say her Son, was in Heaven; her heart then was no longer in herself. [*Matt.* 6:21]. The body that she loved so much, bone of her bone, flesh of her flesh [*Gen.* 2:23], was in Heaven. There she flew, this holy eagle. Wheresoever the body is, there shall the eagles be gathered together. [*Matt.* 24:28, *Douay*]. In short her heart, her soul, her life were in Heaven; how could she remain long on earth? Finally, after so many spiritual flights, after so many suspensions and ecstasies, this holy tower of chastity, this fortress of humility, having miraculously sustained a thousand thousand assaults of love, was carried off and taken captive by a last and universal assault. Love, which was the conqueror, took this beautiful soul away as its prisoner, and left to the sacred body cold death and the tomb. O death, what are you doing in this body? Do you think that you have power to keep it? Do you not remember that the Son of the Lady whose body you possess has vanquished you, defeated you, rendered you His slave? Ah, it is only for a time that He leaves you the glory of this, your victory. [*1 Cor.* 15:55]. You will soon slink away as shamefully as you arrogantly remain there; and love, which by a certain excess allowed you entrance into this holy place, returning in a little while, will deprive you of your possession.

The phoenix dies from the fire, and this holy Lady died of love. The phoenix assembles a funeral pyre of aromatical wood, and placing it on the mountain peak, flaps its wings over this pyre so rapidly that a fire is kindled by the rays of the sun. This Virgin, gathering in her heart the Cross, the crown, the lance of Our Lord, placed them at the summit of her thoughts. Over this pyre she made a great movement of continual meditation, and fire was kindled by the rays of the light of her Son. The phoenix dies in that fire. The Virgin died in this; and it must not be questioned that she had engraven in her heart the instruments of the Passion. Ah, if so many virgins, such as St. Catherine of Siena, St. Claire of Montefalco, had this grace, why not Our Lady, who loved her Son and his death and Cross incomparably more than did ever all the saints together? Indeed, she was nothing but love, and in the

French language the anagram of "Marie" is nothing else but "to love": "aimer" is "Marie," "Marie" is "aimer." Go, then, go, O happy, O beautiful phoenix, burning and dying of love, sleep in peace on the bed of charity!

Thus died the Mother of Life. But as the phoenix rises very soon after its death and assumes a new and happier life, so this Blessed Virgin remained only a brief space of time, no more than three days, before returning to life. Her body, the body which had never experienced any corruption during her holy life, was not subject to corruption after death. Corruption had not tainted such integrity. This ark was of incorruptible wood of acacia [*Ex.* 25:10] like the ancient Ark. Ah, it is believed, as is said in the Book of Revelation [*Rev.* 11:7-11], that the bodies of Elias and Enoch will die, but only for three days, and without corruption. How much more the Virgin, whose immaculate flesh has so intimate a union with that of the Saviour that one could not imagine any imperfection in the one but that the dishonor would reflect on the Other.

You are dirt and to dirt you shall return. That was said to the first Adam and the first Eve. [*Gen.* 3:19]. The second Adam and the second Eve have had no part in that sentence; and that is certainly a universal law, but not without exception, as I have demonstrated with the example of Elijah and Enoch. The whole city of Jericho was sacked and pillaged, but the house of Rahab was privileged and exempt from the sacking because she had lodged the spies of the great Judge Joshua [*Jos.* 6:24-25] for one night. The world and all its inhabitants are subject to the universal sack and pillage and fire; but does it not seem to you only right to exempt Our Lady and her body, the body which received and lodged not spies but the true Joshua, the true Jesus, and not for one night but for many: *Beatus venter, beata ubera.* ["Blessed is the womb, blessed are the breasts"—*Lk.* 11:27]. Worms will eat our bodies, but they reverenced the one which produced the body of their Creator.

The high priest Abiathar had joined in the sedition of

Adonias. Being discovered and apprehended, Solomon said: You ought to die, but because you carried the Ark of the Covenant before my father you shall be spared. [*1 Kgs.* 2:26]. Certainly, according to the universal laws, the Virgin ought not to have been resurrected before the day of the General Resurrection, nor even to have been exempt from corruption. But the honor she had had of carrying before the Eternal Father, not the Ark of the Covenant but His only Son, the Saviour, the Redeemer, rendered her exempt from all these laws. Is it not true that notwithstanding these laws, many arose on the day of the Resurrection—*Multa corpora sanctorum qui dormierant resurrexerunt* ["Many bodies of the saints that had slept arose"—*Matt.* 27:53]. And why not the Virgin, to whom, says the great St. Anselm, we ought not to refuse any privilege or honor which can be accorded to any simple creature.

But finally, if anyone presses me to know what certitude we have for the resurrection of the Virgin, I will respond that we have as much for it as we have for her death. Scripture, which does not gainsay either of these two truths, does not assert either the one or the other in explicit words. But holy Tradition, which teaches us that she was deceased, informs us with equal assurance that she was raised. And if anyone refuses credence to Tradition for the resurrection, who will be able on the same grounds to convince him of her death and burial? But we who are Christians believe, assert, and preach because Tradition supports it, because the Church bears witness to it, that she died and very soon after was brought back to life. And if anyone wishes to gainsay it, we must respond to him as the Apostle did in a like instance: If anyone wants to argue about this, remember that neither we nor the churches of God recognize any other usage. [*1 Cor.* 11:16].

Now it is not sufficient to believe that she was resuscitated, for we must fix firmly in our soul that she was not resuscitated only to die another time, as in the case of Lazarus, but to follow her Son to Heaven, as did those who were raised on the day that Our Lord arose. [*Matt.* 27:53]. The Son who, on coming into this world, received His body and His flesh from His Mother, would not allow His Mother to remain here below, neither in the body nor in the soul. But shortly after she had paid the universal penalty of death, He took her to Himself into the kingdom of His holy Paradise. It is to this that the Church bears witness, calling this feast the "Assumption," based on the same Tradition by which she is assured of Mary's death and resurrection.

Storks have great filial devotion toward their fathers and mothers. When their parents are old and decrepit and the harshness of the season and times compels them to take passage and retreat to a warmer spot, they take hold of their parents, burden themselves with them, and carry them on their wings that they may in some manner reciprocate the benefits they had received from them in their rearing. Our Lord had received His body from that of His Mother. He had been carried for a long time in her sacred womb and in her chaste arms when, because of the harshness of the persecution, it was necessary to take passage and retreat into Egypt. Ah, Lord, said the heavenly court after the death of the Virgin, wake to the judgment You have decreed. [*Ps.* 7:7]. You have commanded that children provide assistance to their aged parents and have embedded this law so deeply in nature that even the storks observe it. Awake to the judgment You have decreed: Permit not that this body which engendered You without corruption now be tainted with corruption in death, but raise it up, and grasping it by the wings of Your power and goodness, carry it from the desert of that lower world to this place of undying happiness.

It must not be doubted that the Saviour willed to observe to the highest point of perfection imaginable this commandment, which He had given to all children. But who is the child who, if he could, would not raise his good mother and place her in Paradise after her decease? This Mother of God died of love, and the love of her Son resuscitated her. And in view of this consideration, which as you see is most reasonable, we say today: Who is this coming up from the desert, leaning upon her Lover? [*Song* 8:5]. It is the subject of our feast. It is the occasion of this great joy which all the saints celebrate in the Church Militant and Triumphant.

When the patriarch Joseph received his good father Jacob into the court of Pharaoh [*Gen.* 47:7] in the kingdom of Egypt, over and above the favorable welcome afforded him by the king himself, there is no doubt that the principal courtiers came before him performing all sorts of most jubilant demonstrations. In the same way, there is no doubt that at the Assumption of the most holy Mother of the Saviour all the angels were festive, celebrating her coming in all manner of joyful songs. Joining our wishes and affections to theirs, we ought to have a solemn feast with exclamations and songs of triumph: Who is this coming up from the desert, flowing with delights? [*Song* 8:5, *Douay*].

And was not this the most beautiful and magnificent entrance into Heaven ever seen, second only to that of her Son? For what soul was ever received there so full of perfection, so richly adorned with virtues and privileges? She comes up from the desert of the lower world, but nevertheless so perfumed with spiritual gifts that, excluding the Person of her Son, Heaven has nothing comparable. She comes up like a column of smoke laden with myrrh, with frankincense: Who is this, it is asked in the Song of Songs, coming up from the desert like a column of smoke, laden with myrrh, with frankincense, and with the perfume of every exotic dust? [*Song* 3:6]. As you know, the Queen of Sheba came to visit King Solomon to consider his wisdom and the beautiful order of his court, and at her arrival she gave him a large amount of gold, spices, and precious stones. Never again did anyone bring such an abundance of spices as the Queen of Sheba gave to King Solomon. [*1 Kgs.* 10:1-2, 10].

But the Virgin, coming up to Heaven into the court of

her Son, brought with her so much gold of charity, so many perfumes of devotion and virtue, such a great quantity of precious stones of patience and sufferings that she had borne in His Name, that reducing them all to merits we can truly say that never was so great a quantity brought to Heaven. Never did anyone present so much to her Son as did this holy Lady.

Do you want further enlightenment on this doctrine? Know that in the matter of good works no one began so early in life nor persevered so diligently as did Our Lady. The rest of us begin quite late, and if we do perform some good works, very often we lose out on them because of sin and inconstancy, so that the sum total is not found to be very much. For, although perhaps we gather some coins in merit, it is only sometimes, and very often we are frivolous and squander our money in one fall into sin. And if by penitence we return to grace, do you not see that we manage our affairs poorly, for we waste very much time. And besides, our strength remains weakened after sin, and even after penitence, so that our store of merits cannot be very great. But let us speak of the more perfect. Even St. John the Baptist, your great patron, O my people, was not exempt from venial sin. Now venial sin tarnishes our works, delays our progress, and impedes our advancement. But our holy Lady was full of grace from her Conception. As soon as she had the use of reason she never ceased to profit and grow more and more in all manner of virtue and graces, so that her accumulation of merits was incomparable: Many daughters have gathered together riches, but you have surpassed them all. [*Prov.* 31:29, *Douay*].

Oh, how she was overflowing with delights, since in this world she had been so rich in good deeds and works! And so she was established in the highest reaches of the glory of the saints. Pharaoh paid such deference to Joseph that when his father arrived in Egypt, Pharaoh said to him: Your father and your brothers have come to you. The land of Egypt is at your disposal. Settle your father and your brothers in the pick of the land. [*Gen.* 47:5-6]. But on this holy day on which Our Lady arrives in the Kingdom of her Son, think what the Eternal Father will say to Him: All My glory is Yours [*Jn.* 17:10], O My Beloved Son. Your Mother has come to You. Have her dwell in the highest reaches, in the best and most eminent place of this Kingdom.

Let us not doubt this, O Christians. When Our Lord came into this world, He sought the lowest place there was [*Eph.* 4:9] and He found none lowlier in humility than the Virgin. Now He raises her up to the highest Heaven in glory. She gave Him a place according to His desire. Now He gives her one according to His love, exalting her above the cherubim and seraphim.

But let us look at the remainder of the sentence we have chosen for our subject. It says that this holy Lady, coming up from the desert flowing with delights, is leaning upon her Lover. This is the last word in all the praises which the Church holily gives to the saints, and above all to the Virgin. For we always refer them to the honor of her Son by whose strength and virtue she ascends to receive the plenitude of delights. Have you not noticed that the Queen of Sheba, in bearing so many precious things to Jerusalem, offered them all to Solomon? Ah, all the saints do the same, and particularly the Virgin. All her perfections, all her virtues, all her happiness are referred, consecrated and dedicated to the glory of her Son, who is their source, their author and finisher [*Heb.* 12:2, *Douay*]: *Soli Deo honor et gloria* ["To the only God be honor and glory"—*1 Tim.* 1:17]. All returns to this point.

If she is holy, who has sanctified her if not her Son? If she is saved, who is her Saviour if not her Son? "Leaning upon her Lover": All her felicity is founded on the mercy of her Son. You would name Our Lady a lily of purity and innocence? Yes, she is that in truth. But this lily has its whiteness from the Blood of the Lamb in which she has been purified, like the robes of those who have washed

them white in the Blood of the Lamb. [*Rev.* 7:14]. If you
call her a rose because of her most excellent charity, her
color will be only the blood of her Son. If you say that she
is a column of smoke, sweet and pleasing [*Song* 3:6], say at
once that the fire of this smoke is the charity of her Son;
the wood is His Cross. In brief, in all and through all she
is leaning upon her Lover. It is in this way, O Christians,
that we must be jealous of the honor of Jesus Christ, not
like the adversaries of the Church who think they honor
the Son by refusing the honor due to the Mother. On the
contrary, the honor borne to the Mother, being referred to
the Son, renders magnificent and illustrious the glory of His
mercy.

To witness to the purity of intention of the Church in the
honor she renders the Virgin, I present to you two contrary
heresies which are opposed to the just honor due to Our
Lady: The one, by excess, named Our Lady a goddess of
Heaven and offered her sacrifice, and this was maintained
by the Collyridians; the other, by default, rejects the honor
Catholics pay to the Virgin, and this was held by the Anti-
dicomarites. Errors always go to extremes and are con-
tradictory to each other.

The Church, which always takes the royal road and
holds to the middle course of virtue, combats the one no
less than the other. Against the one she declares that the
Virgin is only a creature, and henceforth we ought not
offer her any sacrifice. Against the other she asserts that,
nevertheless, this holy Lady, since she is the Mother of the
Son of God, should be recognized as deserving of special
honor—infinitely less than that of her Son, but infinitely
greater than that of all other saints. To the one she reveals
that the Virgin is a creature—but so holy, so perfect, so
perfectly bound, joined and united to her Son, so much
loved and cherished by God that, in truth, one can love the
Son rightly only when for love of Him one has a very great
love for the Mother, and when for the honor of the Son he
pays highest honor to the Mother. But to the other she

says: Sacrifice is the supreme honor of *latria,* which must be offered to God alone as Creator—and do you not see that the Virgin is not the creatrix but only a creature, although a very excellent one?

For myself, I am accustomed to say that in a certain manner the Virgin is more a creature of God and of her Son than is the rest of the universe. God has created in her many more perfections than in all the rest of His creatures, since she was more redeemed than all the rest of humankind, inasmuch as she was redeemed not only from sin but from the power and even the inclination to sin. To purchase the liberty of a person who was to be a slave before she becomes one is a greater grace than to purchase it after she is in captivity. Thus, far are we from attempting to make any one-to-one comparison of the Son with the Mother, as our adversaries believe—or pretend to believe in order to convince the people that we do.

In short, we call her beautiful, and beautiful far beyond all other creatures—but beautiful as the moon [*Song* 6:10], which receives its brightness from that of the sun, for she receives her glory from that of her Son. The thorn called "aspalatus," says Pliny, is not of itself odoriferous, but if the rainbow touches it, it leaves it with an odor of incomparable sweetness. The Virgin was the thorn of that bush, flaming but not burned, which the great Moses saw: In the burning bush which Moses saw we acknowledge your holy virginity [*Ex.* 3:2], says the Church. And assuredly, of herself she was not worthy of any honor, she was without fragrance. But since that great Arc of Heaven, that great sign of the reconciliation of God with men [*Gen.* 9:13-17], came to rest little by little on this holy thorn—first by the grace of her Conception, then by her Motherhood, making Himself her true Son and reposing in her precious womb— its sweetness has become so intense that no other plant has ever had so much: sweetness which is so pleasing to God that the prayers which are perfumed by it are never rejected or useless. But the honor she receives always returns to her Son, from whom she received her fragrance.

Her Son is our Mediator [*1 Jn.* 2:1]; she, our Mediatrix—but in a very different manner, as I have said a hundred times. The Saviour is the Mediator of justice, for He intercedes for us, exposing the right and reason of our cause. He produces our just claims, which are none other than His Redemption, His Blood, His Cross. He acknowledges to His Father that we are debtors, but He shows that He has paid for us. But the Virgin and the saints are mediators of grace. They pray for us that we may be pardoned—all through the mediation of the Passion of the Saviour. They themselves have nothing to show by which we may be justified, but entrust themselves to the Saviour for this. In brief, they do not join their prayers to the intercession of the Saviour, for they are not of the same quality, but to ours.

If Jesus Christ prays in Heaven, He prays in virtue of Himself; but the Virgin prays only as we do, in virtue of her Son, but with more credit and favor. Do you not see that all returns to the honor of her Son and magnifies His glory?

That is why in order to honor Our Lord all antiquity greatly honored His Mother. Look around Christendom: Of three churches, two are under the patronage of the Virgin or are outstanding for the devotion of the people toward her. The daughters of Sion see her. [*Song* 6:9]. The daughters of Sion, the souls of the faithful, the people, have considered her and have praised her for her blessedness. And queens have praised her. [*Song* 6:9]. And not only the people, but the most illustrious personages: Prelates, doctors, princes and monarchs have praised and magnified her. Just as birds begin to chirp at daybreak, each in his own melody, so all peoples bestir themselves to celebrate her honor as she herself has prophesied, saying: All ages to come shall call me blessed. [*Lk.* 1:48]. Consequently, all the faithful, and you most particularly, O Parisians, ought to invoke her and obey her. These are the two primary honors we can render her and she has invited us to render her them.

I find that Our Lady spoke to people only twice according to the account of the Gospel: once when she greeted Elizabeth [*Lk.* 1:40]—and there is no doubt but that at that time she prayed for her, for greetings of the faithful are made by prayer. The second was when she spoke to the servants at the wedding feast in Cana of Galilee, and at that time she said only: Do whatever my Son tells you. [*Jn.* 2:5]. These two acts comprise the exercise of charity and the will of the Virgin regarding us—to pray for us, and consequently we ought to invoke her with great confidence. In all dangers, in all tempests, O Parisians, "Look at this star of the sea, invoke her." With her favor your ship will arrive at port without disaster and without shipwreck.

But if you want her to pray for you, listen to her second word by obeying her commandments. Now her commandments are, in a word, that you do the will of her Son: Do whatever He tells you to do. O Christians, do we desire that the Virgin should hearken to us? Hearken to her. Do you desire that she listen to you? Listen to her. With all her heart and with all the weight of her affections as well, she asks that you be obedient servants of her Son.

One day Bathsheba came to David with many acts of obeisance and reverence in order to make a request and petition. In the end she asked only that her son Solomon be king after his father and succeed him to the throne. [*1 Kgs.* 1:16-17]. This Virgin, O people, asks of you above all, as the most certain demonstration of your devotion to her, that you have her Son for the King of your heart and soul, that He reign in you and that His commandments be carried out. Do this, O people, as your duty, for your salvation, and for love of Our Lady, who, as you have seen, remained for some years yet on earth after the Ascension of her Son. After some time she died of the death of her Son—that is to say, of love. But she did not remain dead for any length of time but was raised up and came up from the desert of this world into Paradise, where she is enthroned above all creatures—and all this for the greater glory of her Son! For this she prays for us, and asks us to be His faithful servants.

O most sacred and most happy Lady, who are in the heights of the Paradise of felicity, alas, have pity on us who are in the desert of misery. You are in the abundance of delights, and we are in the abyss of desolations. Obtain for us the strength to carry our afflictions well and always to be supported by your Lover, the only support of our hopes, the only recompense of our labors, the only medicine of our ills.

Alas, glorious Virgin, pray for the Church of your Son. Assist with your favors all superiors, the Holy Father, prelates and bishops, and particularly those of your city of Paris. Be propitious to the king. Your ancestor David, mindful of the services and offices of Jonathan, was good to Jonathan's son. [*2 Sam.* 9:7]. This king is the descendent of one of your most faithful and devoted servants, the blessed St. Louis. We pray you to grant him your protection in the name of that holy king. May the queen, who has the honor of bearing your name, ever be under the shelter of your holy patronage. O heavenly Lily, stir up the lilies of France with your holy benedictions, that they may always remain white and pure in the unity of true faith and religion. You are a sea. Let the waves of your graces fall on this young dauphin. You are the Star of the Sea. Oh, be propitious to the ship of Paris, that it may arrive at the holy harbor of glory, there to praise the Father, the Son, and the Holy Spirit forever and ever. Amen.

NOTES

1. The expression "O God" or "Oh, my God" is very characteristic of St. Francis de Sales, who lived and spoke in the presence of God.
2. That is, Christ. In this book, the terms "Spouse," "Divine Spouse,"

"Lover," "Divine Lover," and "Beloved" are capitalized when they refer to Christ, and are in lower case when they refer to the Church, to each faithful Christian soul (especially religious), or to the Blessed Virgin Mary—who, as St. Francis de Sales states, merits above all others the name of "spouse" and "lover" of Christ. (Cf. p. 136). Cf. also p. 51-52. The word "divine" here is not always to be taken in the literal sense of referring to God Himself.

— 2 —

OUR LADY OF THE SNOW

Sermon for the Feast of Our Lady of the Snow, August 5, 1617, concerning the origin of this feast, the way to respond to the inspirations of God, imperfect offering of oneself to God, perfect offering of oneself to God by means of the religious life, the way in which snow represents the purity and obedience and fruitfulness of souls in the religious life, and the source of one's happiness in the religious life.

While Our Lord was speaking the words of eternal life [*Jn.* 6:68], a woman rose up from the crowd and said: Blest is the womb that bore You and the breasts that nursed You! [*Lk.* 11:27]. Notice that even though it is our Divine Master who is preaching, this woman begins to praise Our Lady. And yet that is certainly understandable, inasmuch as from devotion to Our Lord is born immediately devotion to His most holy Mother, and no one can love the One without the other. Holy Church is accustomed to having us read this Gospel on feasts of Our Lady, but very particularly today when we celebrate a special one in her honor. It even seems to me that the story which the Church recounts today has a striking comparison to this Gospel.[1]

It is told that there was in the city of Rome a nobleman named John who, since he had no children, desired to consecrate all his wealth to the Divine Majesty, but in honor of Our Lady. His wife was in total agreement. Since they did not know what would be most pleasing to Him, they

began to pray. That night they were both told in a dream
to go to the Esquiline Hill and to have a church built there
in honor of the Blessed Virgin Our Lady, erecting it on the
spot they would find covered with snow. Certainly, a very
great miracle in the month of August and in the city of
Rome, where the heat is so excessive! This very happy
John went to tell his revelation to the Pope and he found
that the latter had received the same sign. After comparing
the three revelations, they visited the place, found the spot,
and then had the church built there. It is still there today
and is called St. Mary Major.

Let us now return to our Gospel. [*Lk.* 11:27-28]. After
this good woman cried out: "Blest is the womb that bore
You and the breasts that nursed You," Our Lord responded: "True"—like one would say: "Yes, indeed! But
still more blest are they who hear the word of God and
keep it," that is to say, who put it into practice. We know
of people who hear the death of the Saviour spoken of and
weep most tenderly, but who nevertheless harbor in themselves a thousand kinds of imperfections contrary to this
holy Passion over which they weep.[2]

You who profess the spiritual life know the difference
between effective love and affective love. Our Lord is not
satisfied with the affective, if we do not also give Him
effective love. Notice that He does not consider those blest
who simply hear His word but only those who also keep it.
God makes it very clear that He does not consider that we
hear His word if we do not put it into effect with the affection of submission and obedience. Thus does He often
complain that His people do not hear Him when He speaks
to them [*Prov.* 1:24; *Is.* 65:12, 66:4; *Jer.* 7:13]; that is to
say, they do not put His words into effect, for they do indeed hear them with their ears. Now that is not sufficient,
for He wants us to listen to them with the intention of making them profitable to ourselves. It is the same when,
speaking of superiors, our Divine Master says: He who
hears you, hears Me. He who rejects you, rejects Me. [*Lk.*

10:16]. It is as if He said: "I consider that those who obey you, obey Me; and I consider that those who reject your words, not wishing to profit by them, reject My words."

On this subject, I remember having explained once from this pulpit what we ought to do in order to profit from hearing the word of God and sermons. I now add that, besides the intention that we ought to have of profiting by it and of giving it our attention, we ought afterwards to remain for some time withdrawn in the depths of our soul, I mean recollected, in order to ruminate on what we have heard. And in order that distractions may not come into our heart and disturb our tranquility, we must do what Solomon did to his Temple. The entire roof was of gold, and he was concerned that birds, by coming to nest and perch upon it, might sully it. Therefore he had it adorned with spikes, thanks to which it could not be damaged. Similarly, if we want to guard our heart against the suggestions and distractions of the evil one, we must, at the end of the sermon, adorn it with aspirations and ejaculatory prayers upon the subject discussed, imploring the Divine Mercy to strengthen us so that we may make effective what our affections approve.

Consider this good man John of whom we are speaking. He was prompt to follow the attraction of God, for being inspired to give Him all his possessions, and not knowing how he could do it for His glory and the honor of Our Lady for whom he had so special a devotion, he began to pray, and understood what he ought to do. Oh! What a good thing is prayer! But the happiness of this holy man did not consist in knowing the will of God, but in immediately following it, as he did. Oh, how happy are they who, being inspired like this blessed John and his wife to dedicate and consecrate themselves to God with all that they possess, have recourse to prayer to learn in what place they should do it for His greater glory and the honor of our most worthy Mistress, for, as we have already declared, there is no devotion for God that is devoid of a desire to please Our Lady.

But who is there, I ask, who would not have an affection for her, seeing that she is our most amiable Mother? And to prove the truth of this, listen to the Spouse in the Song of Songs when He says to her: Your body, O My beloved, is a heap of grains of wheat encircled with the lilies [*Song* 7:3] of its virginal modesty. What does this Divine Lover mean, if not that Our Lady has borne all Christians in her womb—although she produced only that "Grain" of which it is written that unless it falls to the earth it remains just a grain of wheat, but if it falls there and is covered it will germinate and produce many others. [*Jn.* 12:24-25].

To whom, I ask, ought we attribute the production of these other grains if not to her who produced the first one, Our Lord being the natural Son of Our Lady? Although in reality she has borne only Him in her womb, she has nevertheless borne all Christians in the Person of her Divine Son, for this blessed "Grain" has produced us all by His death. Likewise, just as the planted date produces the palm from which a quantity of other dates afterwards come, why can we not say that these dates belong to the first one, from which the palm sprang up?

Blest is the womb that bore You and the breasts that nursed You! We have all been fed from these sacred breasts, for Our Lord nursed and took His nourishment from them, and afterwards fed us from His own. Our most dear Master has the sweetest and most delightful "breasts," as His divine spouse testifies, saying: O my Beloved, how sweet are Your breasts![3] They are more delightful than the wine of all this world's pleasures. [*Song* 1:2]. O God, what honor, love and affection we owe to Our Lady, as much because she is the Mother of our Saviour as because she is also ours!

There are many Christians who insist that they are resolved to dedicate and offer to God all that they have and all that they are, because they know that all belongs to Him, and they would rather die than offend Him mortally.

But it is also true that they want to reserve for themselves the disposal of their goods, and although they are resolved to live in the observance of the commandments of God, they want nevertheless to retain the will to do a great many little things that are not contrary to charity but which incline that way. Those things are dangerous which, although they do not make us lose charity, do however displease the Divine Majesty. God is jealous of our love; that is why He lets His inspirations fall on some souls whom He separates from the rest. With a powerful resolution, these come to consecrate and dedicate their heart with all its affections and their body and all their possessions to His honor and glory, choosing the religious state in order to live there with more perfection and less danger of deviating from their holy resolution and being lost.[4]

This state is certainly the most perfect after that of those who bear the mark of episcopal consecration, inasmuch as one can no longer abandon it. Because of its short duration, martyrdom is not a state and should rather be called a short and fleeting passage, which is not a state. These souls, then, who are so generous as to come to abandon all to God without any reserve, placing themselves under the laws of religion and binding themselves so strictly that they can never dispense themselves from them, act not only like all yellow flowers which always turn toward the sun, but also like that one that is called the "turnsole," or "sunflower." This latter is not content with turning its flower, leaves and stem toward the sun, but by some hidden wonder it also turns its underground root. Thus these blessed souls do not want to turn and abandon themselves to God only by halves, but completely—themselves and all that they have: the leaves of the vain hopes which the world offers, the flower of their purity and the fruits of all that they shall ever do or possess.

They say to Our Lord, in imitation of the great St. Paul: Lord, what is it I must do? [*Acts* 22:10]. And having said this, they submit themselves to the guidance of their superiors, never more to be mistresses of themselves nor of their own will, avoiding in this way the verdict of the great St. Bernard who insists that "he who governs himself is governed by a great fool." Alas, why should we desire to be masters of ourselves in what concerns the spirit when we are not so in what concerns the body? Are we not aware that physicians, when ill, call in other physicians to decide suitable remedies? In the same way, lawyers do not plead their own cause, inasmuch as self-interest usually biases reason.

I now turn to a consideration of why it was not without significance that snow was the sign of the truth of the revelation made to this good man John and his wife. Our Lord could indeed have made manna fall as He did in ancient times in the desert for the Israelites [*Ex.* 16:14], or else He could have covered the spot that He had chosen with the most beautiful flowers, but He did not choose to do so, inasmuch as in the qualities of snow can be recognized the conditions necessary for souls whom He has singled out to be especially His in religion.

First I remark the whiteness of the snow; secondly, its obedience; thirdly, its fecundity. I will pass over its many other properties; it might be said that it never falls on the sea, at least not on the high seas, and I could add that in the same manner, the sacred and special inspiration to give oneself to God without reserve never falls on souls who sail on the high seas of this miserable world and who are there raised to its highest dignities. I know well that there are some, as for example, St. Magdalen, St. Matthew and others, as also a St. Louis and a St. Elizabeth, but all these are rare. Therefore, we can certainly say that if this blessed inspiration falls there, it is only rarely.

We may compare the whiteness of snow to the whiteness of a pure soul because it surpasses any other whiteness, and that this is true you will see in tomorrow's Gospel [*Matt.* 17:1-9], where it is said that Our Lord being transfigured, His clothes became "as white as snow." That shows well enough that nothing whiter can be found. Listen to the royal psalmist David. Lamenting before God that, through sin, his soul has become blacker than black, he entreats Him to be pleased to wash him with His "hyssop" so that by this means it will be made "whiter than snow." [*Ps.* 51:9].

Now, souls divinely called to the religious state are made white as snow, for by the vow of chastity they renounce all the pleasures of the flesh, lawful as well as unlawful, and afterwards receive in exchange the pleasures and satisfactions of the spirit. The holy Prophet said to the Lord: One thing I ask of You, one thing I still seek—that You bring me into Your holy Temple, that I may enjoy there Your loveliness. [*Ps.* 27:4]. It is as if he meant to say that no one will enjoy the dear caresses or the delicious pleasures of Our Lord but those who will renounce all the vain pleasures of the flesh and of the world, since it is not possible to possess both together. It is nevertheless true that the Saviour, having two breasts, nourishes all His children with the mercy that flows from them. There is indeed a certain liquor of mercy which rescues the sinner from his iniquity and pardons him; but His other breast, from which He nourishes the perfect and perfects them more and more, gives forth a liquor "sweeter than honey" [*Ps.* 19:11] and more delicious than nectar and ambrosia; it is all sweetness. Blessed, then, are the souls who renounce absolutely all the delights and pleasures of the flesh that we have in common with the beasts, in order to enjoy those of the spirit which make us like the angels.

Let us pass on to the second quality of snow. I say that it is obedient. It is the divine Psalmist who declares that it is, assuring us that it does the will of God, that it obeys His word. [*Ps.* 148:8]. Ah! Watch it fall: It falls so gently. See how it remains on the ground until it pleases God to send a ray of sunshine which comes to melt it and make it disappear. Oh, how obedient is the snow! Such are souls who dedicate themselves to the Lord, for they are supple and

submit themselves absolutely to the discretion and guidance
of those who command, no longer allowing themselves to
be in control by the use of their own will and judgment.
And just as they have renounced all the pleasures of the
flesh, so do they likewise renounce unreservedly the
pleasure they were accustomed to find in the world by
following the promptings of their own will in all that they
did. Henceforth they will no longer be subject to it, but on
the contrary, they will be subject to the Rules of their Institute. O sweet and loving subjection which makes us
pleasing to God!

In the third place, snow is fruitful. Farmers and those
who till the soil assure us that when there is a moderate
amount of snow in the winter the crops of the following
year will be all the better for it, since the snow protects the
ground from the hard frosts. And although it may seem
that snow, given its coldness, cannot warm the ground, it
still renders it fruitful for the reason just given, for the
grain underneath is well protected. A religious vocation is a
fruitful vocation, inasmuch as it renders the most indifferent actions fruitful and very meritorious. Eating,
drinking, sleeping are things of themselves indifferent and
without any merit. I know well that we must eat and drink
in order to sustain the body, so that being united to the
soul, they can together pass through the course of this life
according to the ordinance of God. Likewise, we must
sleep so that afterwards we may be more vigorous in serving the Divine Majesty. To do all these things in this manner is to obey the great Apostle who says: Whether you eat
or drink—whatever you do—you should do all for the glory
of God. [*1 Cor.* 10:31; *Col.* 3:17]. And certainly, he who
performs these actions otherwise does not live as a Christian but as a beast.

Now, those who are in religion perform all these actions
far more particularly "for the glory of God," inasmuch as
they do them all through obedience. They might indeed be
hungry, but they would not go to eat if the bell did not call

them there; they do not go to eat, then, in order to satisfy their appetite, but they go to eat in order to obey. In the same way they do not go to bed because they are sleepy nor because they must sleep to keep the body vigorous, for if the time has not come, and the bell which is the signal of obedience does not make them go, they will not go at all. Oh, the happiness of being able to obey in all that we do! How great it is!

But do you really know where the happiness of these religious souls comes from? From their obedience to these words which Our Lord spoke to them in the person of His great Prophet David: Hear, O daughter, and see; turn your ear, forget your people and your father's house. [*Ps.* 45:11]. But notice, I pray you, that He is not satisfied that she listens if she does not also turn her ear. This is to show that He wills to be listened to with a particular attention and with affection. But tell us, O holy Prophet, what is the result of all this? The remainder of his discourse tells us: So shall the King desire your beauty [*Ps.* 45:12]; that is, He will make you His beloved spouse and will take His delights in you. Do you see how this obedience contains in itself all the happiness and felicity of these souls? The obedient man, says Holy Scripture [*Prov.* 21:28, *Douay*], will give an account of many glorious "victories" to Our Lord when He comes seated on His judicial throne at the Day of Judgment. [*Matt.* 19:28]. These souls will then speak of "victories" gained not only over themselves, by submitting to obedience, but also of the many they shall have gained over their enemies. And we must not have the slightest doubt but that, having conformed themselves in this life to the obedience of their Master who preferred to die rather than disobey [*Phil.* 2:8], they shall be lovingly received by Him and led to enjoy His glory with Him eternally, toward which the Father and the Son and the Holy Spirit are leading us. Amen. Yes Lord, amen!

NOTES

1. St. Francis de Sales is alluding to the account read in the Office for this feast, a summary of which he now gives.
2. Cf. St. Francis de Sales' *Introduction to the Devout Life*, Part IV, chapter 13. In subsequent notes this work will be referred to as *Introduction*.
3. The New American Bible speaks here of love, rather than breasts.
4. St. Francis is preaching this sermon at the ceremony in which three of the early Visitation Sisters took the religious habit; he moves between the theme of Mary and that of religious life, no doubt underscoring thereby his appreciation of Mary as the perfect model for all states of Christian life.

— 3 —

THE PRESENTATION OF OUR LADY IN THE TEMPLE

Sermon for the Feast of the Presentation of Our Lady, November 21, 1617, concerning Our Lady's childhood, the journey of Mary to Jerusalem with St. Anne and St. Joachim for Mary's Presentation, the renewal of religious vows, God's grace and our cooperation, the total gift of self to God in the religious life, Cain and Abel, and the overcoming of self-will.

Holy Church celebrates today the feast of the Presentation of Our Lady in the Temple. I can say of this feast what is written of the Queen of Saba when she visited Solomon: Never was there seen so much perfume in the city of Jerusalem as she brought with her to offer to this king. [*1 Kgs.* 10:1-2, 10].

Similarly, never was "so much perfume" and ointment offered to God in His Temple as the most holy Virgin brought with her on this day. Never until then had the Divine Majesty received so excellent and pleasing a gift as the offering He received from the blessed St. Joachim and St. Anne. They went to Jerusalem to fulfill the vow they had made to God to dedicate their glorious child to Him in the Temple, where young maidens were brought up for the service of the Divine Majesty.

You can imagine with what fervor this heavenly child longs to leave her father and mother's home to dedicate and consecrate herself more definitively to the service of her heavenly Spouse who attracts and draws her with the fragrance of His perfumes, as the Shulammitess says: O my Beloved, Your name spoken is a spreading perfume—that is why the maidens love You and have gone after You. You are not only perfumed, but perfume itself. [*Song* 1:3-4]. Do you not see that our glorious Lady was longing to see the day when her parents would offer her to God, for it is true that she had the use of reason from the time of her Conception? Certainly we must not believe that this privilege granted to St. John the Baptist was denied to the holy Virgin.

Here is a wonderful, excellent and profitable belief which, because it is to useful, I cannot pass over. The Saviour, being clothed with our humanity, would not depart from the laws of infancy. He grew and performed all His little actions just like all other children, as though He could not do otherwise. Moreover, the holy Virgin and her glorious Son, Our Lord, had the use of reason from their mothers' wombs and were, consequently, endowed with much knowledge. Nevertheless, they concealed it under the law of a profound silence. For, though able to speak from birth, they would not do so, but rather subjected themselves to speak only at the normal time. And the rest of us, who hardly have the use of reason at 40, are so unreasonable that we affect a learned air and speak before we can lisp; and because we wish to appear as savants and sages we cannot conceal our folly. [*Rom.* 1:22]. How amazing! Despite being so self-assured, we cannot talk for long without blundering and making mistakes. Yet we are nevertheless always so eager and quick to speak—even about things of which we know nothing! And then we find it strange that in religion there are times during which silence is imposed and we cannot speak!

This was an act of admirable simplicity on the part of our glorious darling who, while clinging to her mother's breasts, still did not fail to converse with the Divine Majesty. She abstained from speaking till the usual time, and

even then she spoke only as other children of her age,
although she always spoke straight to the point. She remained as a gentle lambkin by the side of St. Anne for
three years, after which she was weaned and brought to the
Temple, there to be offered like Samuel who was led there
by his mother and dedicated to the Lord at the same age.
[*1 Sam.* 1:24-28].

Oh, my God, how I wish I could adequately picture to
myself the sweetness and consolation of this trip from St.
Joachim's home to the Temple of Jerusalem! What content-
ment this little child displayed in seeing that the long-
awaited hour had finally come! Those who went to the
Temple to adore and offer gifts to the Divine Majesty sang
all along the way. The royal prophet David composed a
psalm expressly for this purpose, and Holy Church has us
say it every day in the Divine Office: *"Beati immaculati in
via"*[*Ps.* 119]—"Happy are they whose way is blameless,"
who walk in Your way, Lord, without stain of sin. "In
Your way"—that is to say, in the observance of Your commandments.

The blessed St. Joachim and St. Anne sang this canticle
along the way, and our glorious Lady and Mistress with
them. O God, what melody! How she sang it a thousand
times more sweetly than the angels ever sang. So much
were the angels taken with this that choir after choir of
them came to hear the heavenly harmony. The heavens
opened up and they leaned over the balustrades of the
heavenly Jerusalem to see and admire this darling child. I
mention this in passing in order to give you a subject of
reflection for the rest of the day: the sweetness of this trip.
I also mention this to move you to listen to this divine canticle, which our glorious Princess sings so melodiously,
with the ears of your soul, for St. Bernard calls devotion
the ear of the soul.

Let us come now to our own celebration of today, when
we once again renew and reconfirm our vows.[1] The first
Christians had great spiritual feasts on the anniversary of

their Baptism, which was the day of their dedication—that
is, the day on which they were dedicated to God.[2] They
took no notice of their birthday, for at birth we are not
children of grace, but rather Adamites or children of
Adam. So they celebrated the day on which they were
made children of God—the day of their Baptism.

In like manner, Abraham held a great and solemn feast,
not at the birth of his son Isaac, but on the day of the
child's weaning [*Gen.* 21:8] because, as some say, a baby
is so frail at birth it is not the time for such great joy, given
the danger and peril of death to which infants are subject
at so fragile an age. Others hold that, because the feast was
being held in Isaac's honor, it was quite reasonable that he
should take part in it and eat with the company, which he
had not done before the time when he was five years old.
And it is not unreasonable to have remained so long at his
mother's breast, given the great age to which people then
attained. Or again, and this is the most probable reason,
Abraham prepared this banquet now because at this age he
was able to have greater hopes for his son, inasmuch as at
this age children are given the direction in which they are
to grow up.

It is fitting, then, that every year religious should have a
special feast on the day of their dedication to God and of
their entrance into religion.[3] However, since religious
should not have anything of their own, we have considered
it proper that our sisters celebrate this feast together on the
same day. Every year Holy Church commemorates the
principal actions of our Divine Saviour, of Our Lady and
Mistress, and of many of the saints whom she presents to
us as patrons to imitate. In giving us this particular feast,
she testifies to her desire that at least once every year we
should enter into ourselves and renew the vows and promises made to the Divine Majesty; and especially is this the
case for religious and the rest of us who are dedicated and
consecrated to Him in a special and irrevocable manner.

In our Order we have selected this most appropriate

feast of the Presentation of Our Lady on which to renew our resolutions, to present and offer ourselves to the Divine Majesty under her protection, uniting our own offering with the one she made of herself to God. And in doing this is seen verified the prediction of the great prophet David: Behind her the virgins of her train follow and enter the palace of the king [*Ps.* 45:15-16], to be offered and consecrated in imitation of her as His servants forever. He says that they will come with gladness and joy. Thus, this day which commemorates our dedication to the Divine Goodness is one of joy and consolation. Indeed it really is so, for this day is the more joyful as we have experienced more deeply the sweetness of being entirely dedicated to God.

But when the holy prophet declares that many virgins will be brought after Our Lady, he certainly does not mean to exclude widows, for they will not be rejected from this happy troop for having lost their virginity, since this loss can be repaired by humility. Do you think that those great saints who had been married and who dedicated themselves to the service of the Divine Goodness in their widowhood, such as St. Paula, St. Melanie, St. Frances and so many others, are not of the number of those "virgins"? On the contrary, they have gained by their humility a very glorious virginity. Humility is not only the guardian of virginity, but is also its restorer.

This commemoration of our vows is made principally to strengthen our fervor, to renew our promises, and to reaffirm our good resolutions. As a consummate lute player has the habit of testing the strings of his instrument from time to time to see if they need tightening or loosening in order to render the tone in perfect harmony, so it is necessary at least once a year to examine and consider all the affections of our souls to see if they are in tune so as to sing the canticle of the glory of God and of our own perfection.[4] Thus, annual confessions have been enjoined so that we might discover our strings that are out of tune, our affections that are not really in balance, and our resolutions of the preceding year that have not been kept. After having tightened the pegs of our lute, which are our resolutions, we come with our glorious Lady and Mistress and under her protection, to place all our affections on the altar of the Temple of the Divine Goodness, in order that, without reserve, they may be burned and consumed by the fire of His burning charity.

But since we have preached these past several years on this very day on the subject of the renewal of our souls, let us now turn our discourse to ourselves to see what must be done in order to renew ourselves well. It is a very necessary exercise, since our misery is so great that we always suffer some spiritual loss, and only too frequently fail in our designs. Therefore it is expedient to check ourselves and to consider by what means we can recover what by our weakness, even our negligence, we have lost.

True, we must not be surprised at this, since in this world that is the way it is. Indeed, it seems that even the sun needs to start its course anew once a year, to repair the losses suffered during the year by those places that do not have a favorable climate. Don't you agree that the earth decays during the winter, and when spring comes it has to repair the losses it has suffered during the severe cold? We ought to do the same, making our course like the sun over all the affections and passions of our souls in order to repair the losses caused by their immortification during the year. Then, coming to spring, which is the time of our renewals, we ought to take courage to repair the decay which we have suffered during the wintry time of our lukewarmness.

I consider that in the Presentation of our glorious Mistress there are three points which must be observed in order to make the renovation well. The first is that she comes in her childhood, leaving her parents after being weaned; the second, that she is carried part of the time in her parents' arms and walks the other part with her own feet; the third, that she gives and offers herself entirely, without reserve.

As to the first point, namely, that she came to dedicate herself to God in her early childhood, how can we observe that, inasmuch as we have definitely passed that age and can never more return to it, for time lost cannot be recovered? You say there is no longer a remedy? O pardon me, but there is a remedy for everything! If virginity is restored by humility, and if the chaste widow becomes a glorious and triumphant virgin, why would you hold that we cannot recover time lost by the fervor and diligence with which we use the present time? [*Eph.* 5:15-16]. It is very true that the happiness of those who are dedicated and consecrated to the Divine Majesty from their youth is very great—the more so as God desires it and greatly delights in it [*Eccl.* 12:1], complaining of the contrary when He says through His prophet that people are so perverted from their youth that they have abandoned His way and taken the road to perdition. [*Gen.* 6:5, 8:21; *Is.* 47:13,15].

Infants are neither good nor bad, for they do not yet have the ability to choose either good or evil. During their infancy they walk like those who, upon leaving a town, go straight ahead for some time; but in a little while they come to a fork in the road that divides it in two. It is in their power to take the right or left, according to what seems better to them in order to reach their destination. The Lord wants to indicate that, in like manner, during its infancy humanity followed the path of righteousness, but when it came to a fork in the road it took the left road and has "forsaken Me, the source of living water" [*Jer.* 2:13] and of all blessings, to follow the way of evil.

It is quite certain that the Divine Goodness desires our youth as the most fitting time for us to give ourselves to His service. But do you think that youth is always to be taken and understood in terms of our age, and that the divine spouse means those that are young in years when she says in the Song of Songs that the maidens love their celestial Spouse and are drawn to Him by the fragrance of

His perfumes? [*Song* 1:3-4]. Oh no, without doubt she is speaking of those who are young in zeal and courage and who, in their later years, come to consecrate to the service of His holy love not only every moment of their lives, but all their actions—and this without any reserve. You will say: After we have completed our youth, when is the most fitting time for us to consecrate and devote ourselves to God? Oh, when is it? It is the present moment, now, immediately[5] [*2 Cor.* 6:2]; for the past is no longer ours, the future may never be ours, so the present moment is the best.

What must we do to regain lost time? As I have already said, it must be regained by fervor and diligence in running our course; just as stags that run so lightly, when pursued by the hunter so redouble their speed that they seem to fly, even so should we try to run our course. But at the time of our renovation and reaffirmation we should not only run, but fly, and ask with the holy prophet [*Ps.* 55:7] for the wings of a dove in order that we may fly swiftly, without lagging, until we rest "in the clefts" [*Song* 2:14] of the wall of holy Jerusalem. By this I mean that we should be totally united to Our Lord crucified on Mount Calvary by a perfect conformity of life.

But I have also considered that our glorious Lady and Mistress, coming to dedicate herself to God, was carried by her mother and father a part of the way, and the other part she came on her little feet—always aided, however, by her parents. For when St. Joachim and St. Anne came upon a level stretch, they put her down and allowed her to walk on her own. This little heavenly and glorious child then held up her little fingers to grab hold of her Papa and Mama's hands, lest she trip. As soon as they came upon some rough road, they immediately took her in their arms. They allowed her to walk—not to relieve themselves, because it was a great consolation to carry her, but for the pleasure it gave them to see her taking those little steps.

This is the second remark on the Feast of the Presentation that I want to make, and the second way of imitating our glorious Princess. In order to present ourselves well so as to re-offer to her Divine Son that which we once offered and dedicated to Him—that is, ourselves—we renew our vows, as we have just done. For this custom of renewing our vows can repair any faults we may have committed when we first made them.

During our long pilgrimage on this wretched earth Our Lord leads us in these two ways. He either leads us by the hand, causing us to walk with Him, or He carries us in the arms of His Providence. I mean that He holds us by the hand and lets us walk in the exercise of virtue. For if He did not hold us by the hand it would not be possible for us to travel this road of blessing. And who does not see that usually those who abandon His fatherly hand do not take a single step without tripping and falling head first to the ground. His Goodness is willing to lead us and to carry us, but He also wants us to take our little steps alone, doing on our part all that we can, helped by His grace. And Holy Church, tender and solicitous for her children's well-being, teaches us to pray each day a prayer in which she begs God to accompany us along our earthly pilgrimage and to assist us with His prevenient and accompanying grace, without which we can do nothing.

Leading us by the hand, our Saviour does with us the deeds for which He asks our cooperation. Later He carries us and does in us works altogether performed [by Him], by which I mean that it seems that we do nothing. These are the Sacraments. For, tell me, please, what does it cost us to hear the words, "I absolve you of all your sins," or to receive the Most Holy Sacrament in which is contained all heavenly and earthly delights?[6] [*Wis.* 16:20].

Oh, how happy are the souls who travel through life in this way and leave the arms of the Divine Majesty only to walk and do on their part what they can in the practice of virtue and good works, still always holding on to the hand of Our Lord! For we must not think that we can do any-

thing of ourselves. [*2 Cor.* 3:5]. The spouse testifies to this
clearly in the Song when she says to her Beloved: Draw
me, we will follow You eagerly. [*Song* 1:4]. She says:
"Draw me" to show us that she cannot do anything of herself if she is not drawn and assisted by His loving kindness.
And to show that she desires to correspond to His attraction freely, not through constraint, she adds: "We will run."
Provided You hold out Your hand to us to draw us, we
shall never cease running until You have taken us into
Your arms and we are united to Your Divine Goodness.

Let us pass on now to the third point, which is the absolute surrender of our glorious Mistress to the Divine
Majesty. It is thus that we must give ourselves totally to the
Lord because the Saviour does not want us to do what He
Himself cannot do—which is to give Himself to us par-
tially. His goodness is so great that He wishes to give Himself to us totally. Similarly, He desires, and it is only just,
that we give ourselves to Him without reserve. I know that
people of the world give themselves to God in their
fashion, but I am not speaking of them here—but of us
who are dedicated and consecrated to Him. We must leave
all to have the All which is God. We must forget "our
father's house." [*Ps.* 45:11]. Is this such a great thing?
Isn't it at times more of a consolation than not to do so?
We must give up marriage. O God, all things considered,
what are we giving up? The toil of housekeeping, where,
most often, things go awry or contrary to our will. What
else do we have to give up? Conversations? I am convinced
that ordinarily there is only discontent in them. Either
someone will not honor you as much as you desire or will
not cherish you enough, or someone will say something
that displeases you. In short, the pleasures that are found
in conversations are more often than not displeasing, rather
than pleasing, to us.

But is that all you must give up? Oh, no. There remains
what is most difficult to give up, yourself, your own will. It
must be annihilated entirely, without reserve. I do not say

our self-love, for that will die only when we die, it will live as long as we live; but it is enough if it does not reign in us. It is then self-will which must be destroyed. The thought that we must leave all to become good religious reminds me of a senator who was inspired by God to abandon the world, for he thought that to avoid the perils of the waves of the sea of this miserable world he must put in at the port of monastic life. In fact, he resolved to become a monk and to withdraw into the desert, and he did so. But the poor man wished at the same time to retain some of his attire and maintain some of his worldly connections. Now, what happened to him?

The blessed St. Basil, who loved him very much because of his piety and good life, knowing this, wrote him a letter which contained these words: "O poor man, what have you done? You left the position of senator and the duties of your office, and therefore you are no longer a senator. Yet, you are not a good monk." It is as if he said: "Consider your name, 'monk,' and you will find that it means 'one,' 'alone.'" Now by this word, "alone," I do not understand simply being withdrawn or shut up in a desert. Rather, to be a good monk we must have God alone as the end in all that we do; and *that* is to be alone.

Do you wish to become a good daughter of the Visitation? You must leave all, not only what is outside yourself, but your own self, and be absolutely weaned from self-will, which we tenderly love as if it were our mother. God is not satisfied with our offerings when they are not accompanied by that of our own heart, for He is like the eagle which relishes far more the heart of the birds it takes as prey than the other parts of their body.[7] In the same way, the Divine Majesty asks first for our heart. "My son, give Me your heart" [*Prov.* 23:26], says this incomparable Goodness, and after that your offerings will be pleasing to Me.

The example of Cain demonstrates sufficiently the truth of what we are saying. [*Gen.* 4:3-8]. When he offered his sacrifice, it was not found pleasing to the Divinity, as was his brother Abel's. This was so not only because he had made a bad division [*Septuagint*], offering the smallest and worst of his flock, but also because he had not given his heart. Recognizing this afterwards, he was so miserable that instead of blaming himself for his fault and acknowledging it, he laid hold of poor Abel, whose offering was pleasing to the Divine Goodness because he had first offered himself and only then offered his sacrifice. Cain conceived indignation against his brother because of the great envy he bore toward him. Notice how envy intrudes everywhere. God rebuked him and said to him: "Why are you troubled? If you have offered well there is no reason for it. If your offering is good, but you have not offered it properly, repair your fault." There is a remedy for everything.

Here, then, is the way we must make our sacrifices and offerings to the Divine Goodness. If we wish to be pleasing to Him, we must offer ourselves fully and without any reserve. If, on this day of your renewal of vows, you do that as perfectly as we have just instructed you, in imitation of Our Lady and glorious Mistress, she will lead you to Heaven, and inspire your hearts to sing in this life the *"Laudate Dominum omnes gentes"* ["Praise the Lord, all you nations"—*Ps.* 117], inviting each person to glorify the Divine Majesty. Then you may add: For steadfast is His kindness toward us, attracting us by His goodness to the enjoyment of so many graces and blessings in this perishable life, so that afterwards we may sing eternally in Heaven in the company of our most holy Mistress and the saints: Glory to the Father and to the Son and to the Holy Spirit. Amen.

NOTES

1. From 1615 on, the Sisters of the Visitation renewed their vows on the Feast of the Presentation. That tradition continues today, not only in the Visitation Order but among many other religious as well.

2. *Introduction,* V, 2.
3. To "enter religion" means to make the three vows of poverty, chastity and obedience in a religious order. The making of these vows on the day of religious profession has traditionally been considered a "second Baptism" which wipes from the soul all sin and all debt of temporal punishment due to sin.
4. St. Francis de Sales proves himself once again an excellent psychologist, affirming as he does the need for people to renew and re-own vows, promises and resolutions from time to time. He insists that relationships not be placed on "automatic pilot"—above all, our relationship with God. One can find similar advice in his *Introduction to the Devout Life,* Part V.
5. St. Francis might easily be considered a Christian existentialist by the emphasis he gives in his spirituality to the present moment. The past is gone and the future is not yet. God speaks to us now. Therefore, we must be docile to His will at this present moment.
6. St. Francis de Sales is dealing here with subtle issues in the theology of grace. His position is clear. Divine grace has absolute priority: It precedes, accompanies and perfects all our deeds. Yet, God in His grace invites and enables human cooperation.
7. *Introduction,* III, 18.

— 4 —

THE VISITATION

Sermon for the Feast of the Visitation, July 2, 1618, concerning Our Lady's motives for visiting St. Elizabeth, Our Lady's charity, her humility and how this humility pleased God, the blessings which came to the house of Zechariah at Mary's visitation, St. Elizabeth's prophecy and Mary's response, and the imitation of Our Lady by the Sisters of the Visitation.

"Thereupon Mary set out, proceeding in haste into the hill country to a town of Judah."—Lk. 1:39

Our most lovable and never-sufficiently-loved Lady and Mistress, the glorious Virgin, had no sooner given her consent to the words of the angel Gabriel than the mystery of the Incarnation was accomplished in her. Upon hearing from the same holy Gabriel that her kinswoman Elizabeth had in her old age conceived a son [*Lk.* 1:36], she desired, being her relative, to go to see her, so that she might wait upon her and be a comfort to her during her pregnancy, for she knew that such was the divine will. And, says the Evangelist St. Luke, she immediately left Nazareth, the little town of Galilee where she lived, to go into Judea to the house of Zechariah. *Abiit in montana:* She went up into the hill country of Juda and set out upon the journey, though it was long and difficult; for, as many authors remark, the town where Elizabeth dwelt is 27 leagues distant from

48

Nazareth; others say a little less, but in any case it was a rough enough road for this weak and delicate Virgin, because it was mountainous.

Thus, aware of a divine inspiration, she started out. She was not drawn by any curiosity to see if what the angel had told her was really true, for she had not the least doubt about it, but rather she was quite certain that things were exactly as he had declared. Still, some persons have chosen to maintain that she was, to a certain extent, moved by curiosity in her resolution; for it is true that it was an unheard-of wonder that St. Elizabeth, who had never had any children, and who was barren, should have in her old age conceived. Or else, say they, it may be that she had some doubt with regard to what the angel had announced to her—which is not true, and St. Luke condemns and refutes them by the words which he writes in his first chapter: that St. Elizabeth, seeing the Virgin enter, exclaimed: Blest is she who trusted that the Lord's word to her would be fulfilled. [*Lk.* 1:45]. It was not therefore curiosity nor any doubt as to the pregnancy of St. Elizabeth which made her undertake this journey, but rather many desirable motives, of which I will mention a few.

She went in order to see that great wonder, or that great grace, which God had worked on behalf of this good old and barren woman, that she should conceive a son in spite of her barrenness, for she knew well that in the Old Law it was a subject of reproach to be childless; but because this good woman was old, she also went that she might be of service to her during this time of her pregnancy, and offer her all the help she possibly could. Secondly, it was in order to tell her of the exalted mystery of the Incarnation which had been worked in her; for Our Lady was not unaware that her kinswoman Elizabeth was a just person [*Lk.* 1:6], very good, and God-fearing. She also knew that she ardently desired the coming of the Messiah, promised in the Law for the Redemption of the world, and that it would be an immense consolation for her to know that the divine promises were fulfilled and that the time desired by the patriarchs and prophets had already come. Thirdly, she also went to restore Zechariah's speech which was lost through his disbelief in the prediction of the angel when he told him that his wife would conceive a son who was to be called "John." [*Lk.* 1:13, 18-20]. Fourthly, she knew that this visit would draw down an immense number of blessings upon the house of Zechariah, superabundant blessings, which would penetrate even to the child in the womb of St. Elizabeth, who would be sanctified through her coming. Such were her motives, as well as many others which I could mention; but I would never finish!

Do you not think after all, my very dear Sisters, that what most especially led our glorious Mistress to pay this visit, which made her travel with that promptitude and in all haste into the hill country of Judah, was her most ardent charity and a most profound humility? Oh, most certainly, my dear Sisters, it was these two virtues which motivated her, and made her leave her little Nazareth, for charity is never idle; it burns in the hearts where it dwells and reigns, and the most blessed Virgin was full of it, because she bore Love Itself in her womb. She made continual acts of love, not only for God with whom she was united by the most perfect charity possible; she also loved her neighbor in a most perfect degree, which made her ardently desire the salvation of the whole world and the sanctification of souls; and knowing that she could cooperate with that of St. John, still in the womb of St. Elizabeth, she went there in all haste. Her charity urged her to rejoice with this good and venerable woman whom the Lord had blessed with such a benediction that, from being childless and barren, she had conceived and now was carrying him who was to be the Precursor of the Incarnate Word.

She went therefore to rejoice with her kinswoman, and that they might mutually help one another give glory to God, who had lavished such graces upon both: upon her who was a virgin, causing her to conceive the Son of God through the operation of the Holy Spirit [*Lk*. 1:35], and upon St. Elizabeth who was barren, making her conceive miraculously and through a special grace him who was to be the Precursor of the Messiah. But as it would have been unfitting that he who was chosen to prepare the way of the Lord [*Lk*. 1:76] should be stained with sin, Our Lady went quickly that he might be sanctified, and that this sacred Child who was God, to whom alone belongs the sanctification of souls, might during this visit bring it about in the glorious St. John, purifying him and delivering him from Original Sin. This He did with such plenitude that many Doctors unhesitatingly affirm that St. John never sinned even venially, although some others hold the contrary opinion.

It was charity, therefore, which made the Most Blessed Virgin cooperate in this sanctification. But it is no wonder that her sacred heart was quite full of love and desire for the salvation of people, since she bore within her chaste womb Love Itself, the Saviour and Redeemer of the world; and it seems to me that it is to her that these words of the Song of Songs should be applied: Your head rises like Carmel. [*Song* 7:6].

See, when the Divine Spouse describes the beauty of His spouse in detail, He begins with her head. But what does this Divine Lover mean when He says that the head of His beloved rises like Carmel? Mount Carmel is covered with a variety of sweet-smelling flowers, and the trees which grow there are full of perfumes. What do these flowers and perfumes represent if not charity, which is a most beautiful and fragrant virtue, one which never dwells alone in a soul? And although these words of the Song of Songs are applied to the Church, the true spouse of Our Lord, in which, as on Mount Carmel, abound all kinds of flowers of virtues and which is fragrant with holiness and perfection, still the same may be understood also of the Blessed Virgin, who is the faithful spouse of the Holy Spirit. Possessing this charity therefore in such great perfection, she resembled

Mount Carmel because of the frequent acts of this virtue
which she made toward God, as well as toward the neighbor; and this charity, like a sweet-scented tree, gave forth a
most pleasant perfume and fragrance.

The rabbis and some others seem to make it more clearly
understood that the Divine Spouse, speaking of the head of
His beloved, means to signify charity; for they render it
thus: "Your lips are like a scarlet strand." And in another
passage the cheeks of the spouse are compared to the seeds
of the pomegranate [*Song* 4:3, 6:7], which are quite red.
And what is the meaning of all this but that it plainly
represents the charity of the Blessed Virgin? For she not
only possessed charity, but had received it in such
plenitude that she was charity itself. She had conceived
Him who, being all love, had transformed her into love itself; so much so that to her, more fittingly than to any
other, may be applied those words of the Song of Songs
which the Sacred Spouse said when, beholding His beloved
in her sweet repose, and seized with a holy delight, He ad-
jured the daughters of Jerusalem not to awaken her, saying:
I adjure you, daughters of Jerusalem, by the gazelles and
hinds of the field, do not arouse My love who is in love,
nor stir up love before its own time. [*Song* 2:7, 3:5]. And
why? Because she is in charity and in love. Or rather, according to another version:[1] I adjure you, daughters of
Jerusalem, not to awaken dilection and love itself, until she
wishes; and this dilection and love is My beloved, that is to
say the Blessed Virgin, who not only possesses love, but is
love itself. She it is whom God has looked upon with a
quite special complacency; for who could have been such a
cause of delight to Our Lord but the one who possessed all
virtues in perfection? Along with charity, she was gifted
with a profound humility, as is testified by those words
which she uttered when St. Elizabeth praised her. Because
God has looked upon His servant in her lowliness, all ages
to come will praise her and call her blessed. [*Lk.* 1:48].

But in order to free our minds from all cause of perplexity, let us explain how these words should be understood. Many Doctors think that when Our Lady said that Our Lord had looked upon His servant in her lowliness, she did not mean to speak of the virtue of humility which she possessed. Among those who hold this opinion we find Maldonat and others; for, they add, although the Virgin possessed a most profound humility, still she did not think herself humble; still less would she wish to speak of humility, inasmuch as the very word would have been contrary to humility itself. But when she said: "He has looked upon His servant in her lowliness," she meant the baseness, misery and abjection which she beheld in herself, and which were natural to her and to the nothingness whence she came. It was thus that she declared that God had looked upon His servant in her lowliness; for they who are truly humble, say these Doctors, never either see or believe that they have the virtue of humility.

Others hold the contrary opinion, which is the more probable; they think that Our Lady meant to speak of the virtue of humility, and that she knew well that it was this virtue which had drawn the Son of God into her womb. There is no doubt, therefore, about her knowing that she possessed this virtue, and this without danger of losing it, because she acknowledged that the humility which she saw in herself was not of her. Did not the great Apostle St. Paul protest that he possessed charity, and this in words so confident that he seems to speak with more presumption than humility? He said: Who will separate me from the love of Christ? [*Rom.* 8:35-39]. Shall it be chains, troubles, death, the cross, fire, the sword? No, nothing will be able to separate me from the love of God that comes to me in Christ Jesus.

Do you see with what boldness this Apostle speaks? If he protests that nothing will separate him from the love of his God, he must necessarily believe that he possesses charity. Indeed, there is no doubt about it, although when he says: Who will separate me from the love of my God?

we must take it for granted that he means with the help of God's grace. Thus the glorious Virgin did not fail at all in humility, nor did she commit any fault contrary to it when she declared that God had looked upon His servant in her lowliness, any more than St. Paul did when he exclaimed: Who will separate me from love? Our Lady knew that this virtue of humility touches and attracts the Heart of God more than all others.

After having considered His spouse in detail, the Spouse in the Song of Songs takes notice of her shoes and of her manner of walking, which pleased Him so much that He acknowledges Himself to be quite charmed by them. Oh, He exclaims, your sandals are pleasing to Me! How beautiful are your feet! [*Song* 7:2]. We read likewise in Holy Scripture that when Judith went to visit Holofernes she was beautifully dressed [*Jdt.* 10:3-4, 16:7-9]; her face was the loveliest imaginable, her eyes glistened, and her lips were like rubies, her hair loose and falling over her shoulders. Nevertheless, Holofernes was ravished neither by the eyes, nor by the lips, nor by the hair of Judith, nor by anything I have mentioned regarding her; but when he fixed his eyes on her sandals and shoes, which, as we may imagine, were embroidered with gold in a most artistic manner, he was completely charmed and overcome. Thus Our Lord saw indeed the variety and beauty of the virtues of Our Lady, which made her extremely beautiful, but when the Eternal Father cast His eyes upon her sandals or shoes, He was so ravished that He allowed Himself to be overcome, and sent her His Son, who became incarnate in her most chaste womb.

And what are these sandals and these shoes of the Virgin but her humility, which is represented by shoes, the humblest garments made use of for the adornment of the body, since they always touch the ground and tread upon mud and dirt. Thus it is the characteristic of true humility to be ever lowly, little, and at the feet of everyone. This virtue is the basis and foundation of the spiritual life, for it always chooses to be on the ground, with its nothingness and abjection. It is this lowliness which God had looked at in the Blessed Virgin, and from this look proceeded all her happiness; therefore she says, because of that she will be proclaimed blessed by all creation, from generation to generation. Our Lady then, when she said that God had looked upon her lowliness, reflected upon herself, upon her nature and upon her being; the result was that she humbled herself.

Abraham, whose faith was so great, was not unaware of God's gifts to him. He declares, nevertheless, as it is written in Genesis, that he is only dust and ashes. [*Gen.* 18:27]. And Our Lord says of Himself[2] that He is more worm than man. [*Ps.* 22:7]. Thus the Blessed Virgin, reflecting upon her most pure and holy life, saw that it was good; and seeing humility in herself, she can in this sense say that God has looked upon her humility; but also, in the other sense, seeing her nothingness, she can say that He has looked upon her lowliness, her worthlessness and her abjection, and for that reason she should be called blessed.

Now in either sense, she spoke with such deep humility that it was evident that she considered all her happiness to consist in the fact that God had cast His eyes upon her littleness, and therefore we may apply to her these words of the Song of Songs [1:12]: For the King's banquet my nard gives forth its fragrance. [And the King replies:] To Me My beloved is a nard which sends forth a most pleasant fragrance.

The nard is a small shrub which exudes a very sweet perfume; it does not rise high like the cedars of Lebanon, but remains in its lowliness, exhaling its perfume with such sweetness that it delights all those who smell it. The holy and most sacred Virgin was this precious nard who never exalted herself on account of anything that was said or done to her; but in her lowliness and littleness, like nard, she gave forth a perfume of such sweet fragrance that it rose to the throne of the Divine Majesty, who was so charmed and delighted by it that He left Heaven to come down here upon earth and become incarnate in the most pure womb of this incomparable Virgin.

You see then, my very dear Sisters, how pleasing humility is to God, and how our glorious Mistress was chosen to be the Mother of Our Lord because she was humble. Even her Divine Son gave testimony of this. When that good woman, seeing the miracle He had just worked, and noticing the murmuring of the Jews, rose up and cried out with a loud voice: Blest is the womb that bore You and the breasts that nursed You, the Saviour made answer: Rather, blest are they who hear the word of God and keep it! [*Lk.* 11:27-28]. It is as though He meant to say: It is true that My Mother is indeed blessed because she bore Me in her womb; but she is far more so because of the humility with which she has heard the words of My heavenly Father and has kept them. And another time, when they came to tell Him that His Mother was asking for Him, this Divine Master replied that those there who did the will of His Father were His Mother, His brothers and His sisters. [*Matt.* 12:47-50]. It is not that He did not wish to recognize His Mother, but He wanted to make it understood that she was pleasing to God not only because she had borne Him in her womb, but still more because of the humility with which she fulfilled His will in all things.

But I see that the time is getting on so I will finish by filling up the few remaining minutes with the rest of this Gospel account, for it is extremely beautiful and must be, I think, most delightful to listen to. The Evangelist says that the Virgin proceeded in haste and went up into the hill country of Juda, to show the promptitude with which we should respond to divine inspirations; for when the Holy Spirit touches a heart, He puts to flight all tepidity: He loves diligence and promptitude, and is the enemy of procrastination and delays in the performance of the divine will. Mary set out *(Exsurgens Maria);* she rises up promptly and proceeds in haste into the hill country of Juda, for the

Child whom she bore within her did not inconvenience her
in the least, inasmuch as He was unlike others; therefore
the Virgin felt not the inconvenience of other women, who
are heavy and unable to walk on account of the weight of
the child they bear, because these children are sinners.[3]
But Our Lady's Child was no sinner; rather, He was the
Saviour of sinners and He who came to take away the sin
of the world. [*Jn.* 1:29]. Therefore He did not burden her,
but only made her lighter and more active. Another reason
why she walked quickly was that her virginal purity urged
her to do so in order that she might soon be in seclusion,
for virgins should remain hidden and appear as little as
possible amidst the bustle of the world.

Intravit Maria. She entered Zechariah's house and
greeted her cousin Elizabeth [*Lk.* 1:40]; she kissed and
embraced her. See how I am hurrying over our Gospel, for
it is time to stop. St. Luke says clearly that Mary greeted
Elizabeth, but as to Zechariah he is silent, because the
virginity of Our Lady did not allow her to greet men, and
she wished to teach us that virgins cannot be too careful in
guarding their purity. There are a thousand beautiful in-
structions on all these things, but I am passing them over,
and just finishing this account. What graces and favors,
think you, my dear Sisters, must have descended upon
Zechariah's house when the Virgin entered it? If Abraham
received so many graces for having given hospitality to
three angels in his tent [*Gen.* 18]; if Jacob drew down so
many blessings upon Laban [*Gen.* 29], although this latter
was a bad man; if Lot was delivered from the burning of
Sodom because he had given a lodging to two angels [*Gen.*
19]; if the prophet Elisha[4] filled all the poor widow's
vessels; if Elisha raised to life the child of the Shunammite
[*2 Kgs.* 4:8-37]; in brief, if Obed-edom received so many
favors from Heaven for having sheltered in his house the
Ark of the Covenant [*2 Sam.* 6:10-11; *1 Chr.* 13:13-14],
what graces and how many heavenly blessings must have
descended upon the house of Zechariah into which entered

the Angel of the Great Counsel [*Is.* 9:5, *Septuagint*], that true Jacob and Divine Prophet, the true Ark of the Covenant, Our Lord enclosed within the womb of Our Lady!

Indeed, the whole house was overcome with joy; the infant leapt with joy, the father recovered his speech, the mother was filled with the Holy Spirit and received the gift of prophecy, for on seeing this blessed Lady enter her house she exclaimed: Who am I that the Mother of my Lord should come to visit me? [*Lk.* 1:41-44, 64]. You see, she calls her "Mother" before she has given birth to the Child. This is contrary to the ordinary custom, inasmuch as we never call women "mothers" before the birth of their children, because they often give birth by miscarriage. But St. Elizabeth knew well that the Virgin would have a happy childbirth, and therefore she does not hesitate to call her "Mother" before she is such in reality, for she is certain that she will be one, and not only Mother of a man, but also of God, and consequently that she will be Queen of men and angels. This is why she is astonished that such a princess should have come to visit her.

Then she said: Blest are you, my Lady, who believed; and moreover, blest are you above all women. [*Lk.* 1:45, 42]. We see by this in what degree she received the gift of prophecy, for she speaks of things past, present and future. "Blest are you who believed all that the angel told you, because you have shown thereby that you have greater faith than Abraham. [Cf. *Gen.* 17:17]. You have believed that the virgin and the barren would conceive, which is something that exceeds the course of nature." See what she knows of the past, through the spirit of prophecy. Regarding what is to come, she sees by this same spirit that the Virgin will be blest among all women, and she proclaims it. She speaks also of the present, calling her "Mother of God." Again, she adds that the child which she bears leapt for joy at her arrival.

It is, indeed, no wonder that St. John leapt for joy at the coming of his Saviour, since Our Lord said, speaking to the

Jews: Your father Abraham rejoiced when, with the eyes of prophecy, he saw My day come, which you now see. [*Jn.* 8:56]. And if all the prophets desired the Messiah promised in the Law and rejoiced because they knew that all would be fulfilled in His day, how much more should we think that St. John was filled with gladness when he saw from his mother's womb the true promised Messiah, the Desired of the patriarchs [*Agg.* 2:8, *Douay*], who had come to visit him in order to begin in him the work of our Redemption by freeing him from the stain of Original Sin!

Oh, my very dear Sisters, how you should be overwhelmed with joy when you are visited by this Divine Saviour in the Most Blessed Sacrament of the Altar, and by the interior graces which you receive daily from His Divine Majesty through the many inspirations and words which He speaks to your hearts. For He is ever near them, knocking, and speaking to you [*Rev.* 3:20] of what He desires you to do for His love. Ah! What thanksgiving you owe to this Lord for so many favors! With what careful attention you should listen to Him, and how faithfully and promptly you should do His divine will!

The most holy Virgin, hearing what her kinswoman Elizabeth said in her praise, humbled herself and referred all the glory to God. Then declaring that all her happiness, as I said, came from the fact that He had looked upon His servant in her lowliness, she entoned that beautiful and wonderful canticle, the Magnificat [*Lk.* 1:46-55], a canticle surpassing all those which had been sung by other women: It was more excellent than that of Judith [*Jdt.* 16:1-17], more beautiful beyond compare than the one which the sister of Moses sang after the children of Israel had passed through the Red Sea and Pharaoh and the Egyptians had been swallowed up in its waters. [*Ex.* 15:1-21]. It was, in short, more beautiful than that sung by Simeon [*Lk.* 2:29-32] or any others of which Scripture makes mention.

O my dear Sisters, you who claim this Virgin for your Mother, daughters of the Visitation of Our Lady and of St.

Elizabeth, what zeal you should have in imitating her, especially her charity and humility, which were the chief virtues which urged her to make this visitation.[5] You should therefore be particularly distinguished in their practice, which will move you to go with haste and joy to visit your sick sisters, cordially helping and serving one another in your infirmities, whether they be spiritual or corporal. And whenever there is an opportunity of practicing humility and charity you ought to do so with a special care and promptness; because, you see, to be a daughter of Our Lady it is not enough to rest content with living in a convent of the Visitation and wearing the religious veil. This would be wronging such a Mother; to be satisfied with this would be to degenerate. You must imitate her holiness and her virtues.

Oh, then, my dear Sisters, be most careful to model your lives on hers: Be meek, humble, charitable and kind, and magnify the Lord with her during this life. And if you do so humbly and faithfully in this world, you will undoubtedly sing the Magnificat in Heaven, with the Virgin herself; and praising the Divine Majesty by means of this sacred canticle, you will be blessed by Him for all eternity, to which the Father and the Son and the Holy Spirit are leading us. Amen.

NOTES

1. St. Francis is using another version of the Song of Songs here. The Annecy edition has "Hebrew, Syrian, Arabic" in the margin.
2. St. Francis de Sales is following the New Testament's lead in seeing this psalm as applying to Jesus, the Messiah, in His sufferings for our salvation.
3. St. Francis is alluding to the condition of Original Sin.
4. *2 Kgs.* 4:1-7; cf. a similar incident in Elijah's life in *1 Kgs.* 17:10-16.
5. St. Francis is deliberately using the word "visitation" rather than "visit" in deference to his congregation, the Order of the Visitation of Holy Mary, which was named after this event in the Gospel.

— 5 —

THE ASSUMPTION
OF THE BLESSED VIRGIN MARY

*Sermon for the Feast of the Assumption, August
15, 1618, concerning Our Lady's fulfillment of
the roles of both Martha and Mary, Our Lady's
glorious death and reception into Heaven, what
Our Lord won by His conquest of the devil, the
envy and anxiety of Martha, how not to be anxious in the practice of virtue, and the reward
which the Eternal King gave Our Lady when she
entered Heaven.*

Today Holy Church celebrates the feast of the glorious
death or falling asleep of the most holy Virgin, and her
Assumption. Many have called this feast by different
names: Some call it the Assumption, others the Coronation
of Our Lady, and others her reception into Heaven. There
are a thousand considerations that could be made on this
subject, but I will limit myself and speak of only two,
namely, how this sacred Virgin received Our Lord and
Master when He descended from Heaven to earth, and how
her Divine Son received her when she left earth to go to
Heaven.

The Gospel which we heard proclaimed at today's Mass
[*Lk.* 10:38-42] furnishes us with sufficient matter for both
propositions. This Gospel tells us that Our Lord, passing
through a village named Bethany, entered a home which
belonged to a woman named Martha, who had a sister
named Mary Magdalene.[1] Martha was busy, eagerly pre-

paring dinner for Our Lord, while Mary seated herself at His feet and listened to His words. Martha wanted everyone to be as solicitous to serve the Saviour as she was. So she complained to Him, and asked Him to order her sister to help her, for she thought it unnecessary for anyone to remain near Him because He knew well enough how to entertain Himself. But our Divine Master reproved her, telling her that she was anxious and upset about many things, and added: One thing only is required. Mary has chosen the better portion and she shall not be deprived of it.

These two women represent Our Lady: Martha, in the reception which the sacred Virgin gave to her Divine Son and the care she bestowed on Him while He was in this mortal life; Mary, in the reception given her by her Son in His heavenly glory.

Our Lady performed the duties of both these sisters admirably in this life. O God! What care did she not take to provide all that Our Lord needed while He was little! What eagerness, or to speak more correctly, what diligence did she not employ in order to avoid Herod's anger! What did she not do to save Him from the many dangers and misfortunes which threatened Him!

But notice, please, how excellently she practiced the role of Mary [in today's Gospel]. The holy Gospel makes special mention of the silence of Our Lady. [*Lk.* 2:51]. Mary was silent and seated herself at the feet of her Master. She had no care but to enjoy His presence. It seems that our worthy Mistress had only this one care. Picture her in the city of Bethlehem where, after every effort is made to find her a lodging and none is found, she says not a word. She enters the stable, brings forth her Beloved Son, and lays Him in a manger [*Lk.* 2:7]. The Kings come to adore Him, and we may imagine what praises they offer to the Child and the Mother; but she speaks not a word. She carries Him into Egypt. She brings Him back, without speaking either to express her sorrow in taking Him there or the joy she must have felt in bringing Him back. But what is still more admirable, see her on Mount Calvary [*Jn.* 19:25-27]: She does not yield to outbursts of grief, nor does she utter a single word. She is at the feet of her Son and that is all she desires. It is as if she is perfectly indifferent. She seems to say: "Whatever may happen, provided I am always near Him and possess Him, I am satisfied, since I desire and seek only Him."

Notice, please, that Our Lord reproved Martha because she was anxious and not because she was careful. Our Lady took great care in serving our Divine Master, but a care which was free of trouble and anxiety. The saints in Heaven are careful to glorify and praise God, but without anxiety, for they can have none. The angels are solicitous for our salvation, and God Himself is full of care for His creatures, but with peace and tranquility. The rest of us are so miserable that we rarely have care without anxiety and upset. You will often see a man who has a great love for preaching. Forbid him to preach and you will see him troubled. Another who would like to visit and console the sick will not do so without anxiety and is even upset if he is prevented. Another has a great love for mental prayer, and although it seems that this regards only the spirit, nevertheless he fails not to be anxious and troubled if he is called away from it to do something else.

Tell me now, if Martha's only care had been to please Our Lord, would she have been so busy? Certainly not, for a single dish, well prepared, was sufficient for His nourishment, seeing that He would have had more pleasure in her listening to Him as Mary did. Martha, along with the intention and desire of providing what was necessary for her Master, had also a little self-esteem which prompted her to display the courtesy and affability with which she received those who did her the honor of visiting her, devoting herself entirely to the service proper for the exterior treatment of the Saviour. In this the good woman thought herself a good servant of God, and she esteemed herself as something. And because she greatly loved her sister, she wished her to be, like herself, eager to serve her most dear Master. Yet He took more pleasure in the attention of Mary, into whose heart He distilled, by means of His words, greater graces than we can imagine.

This corresponds to the answer He gave to the woman who is mentioned in the Gospel [*Lk.* 11:27-28]: You say well that blest is the womb that bore Me and the breasts that nursed Me; but I say to you that blest are they who hear the word of God and keep it.

Those persons who, like Martha, are desirous and anxious to do something for Our Lord think they are very devout and believe that this eagerness is a virtue. However, it is not so, as He Himself gives us to understand: One thing only is required, that is, to have God and to possess Him. If I seek only Him, what does it matter to me if I have to do one thing or another? If I desire only His will, what will it matter to me whether I am sent to Spain or to Ireland? And if I seek only His Cross, why shall I be troubled if I am sent to the Indies, to old countries or to new, since I am certain that I shall find it everywhere?

Finally, our glorious Mistress performed the office of Martha, receiving Our Lord into her home and into her very womb, with extreme affection and devotion. She served Him with such care during the whole course of His life that nothing can be compared to it. It remains to be seen how her Son, in exchange, received her into Heaven. It was with an incomparable love and glory, with a magnificence as much above all the saints as her merits surpassed all theirs.

But before speaking of her reception into Heaven, I must tell you how and by what manner of death she died.[2] You all know the history of her glorious death. Yet I always feel urged to dwell upon the mysteries we celebrate. Our Lady and most worthy Mistress died at 63, or rather fell asleep in the sleep of death. Some will wonder at this and say: How is it that Our Lord, who loved His Holy Mother so tenderly and so deeply, did not grant her the privilege of not dying? Since death is the penalty for sin and she had never committed any, why did He permit her to die?

O mortals, how different are your thoughts from those of the saints, how distant are your judgments from those of the Divine Majesty [Cf. *Is.* 55:8-9]: Do you not know that death is no longer ignominious but precious [*Ps.* 116:15], since Our Lord and Master allowed Himself to be attacked by it on the tree of the Cross. It would not have been an advantage nor a privilege for the Holy Virgin not to die, for she had desired death since she saw it in the arms and in the very heart of her most sacred Son. Death is so sweet and so desirable that the angels would consider themselves happy if they could die. And the saints have rejoiced to suffer death, which gave them much consolation, because our Divine Saviour who is our Life [*Col.* 3:4] had abandoned Himself as a prey to death.

It is generally said that as the life has been, so is the death. By what death, then, do you think the Holy Virgin died if not by the death of love? O it is unquestionable that she died of love, but I do not say this because it is written. She was always the Mother of fair love. [*Ecclus.* 24:24, *Douay*]. No raptures or ecstasies are mentioned in her life because her raptures were continual. She loved with a love which was always strong, always ardent but tranquil, accompanied by great peace. And although this love was continually increasing, it did not increase by transports and outbursts; but like a gentle river it was always flowing, almost imperceptibly, toward that union, so longed for, of her soul with the Divine Goodness.

When the hour came for the most glorious Virgin to leave this life, love made the separation of her soul from her body, death being only this separation. Her most holy soul went immediately to Heaven. For what, I ask, could have prevented it, since she was all pure and had never contracted the least stain of sin? What prevents the rest of us from going directly to Heaven when we die, as Our Lady did, is that almost all of us have dust or stains on our feet which must be washed away and purified in that place called Purgatory before we enter Heaven.

The great men of this world often have assemblies which for the most part are simply useless. They fancy that their meeting place should not be bright, but dark and dimly lighted so that some ballet, or I know not what, may be performed which will appear to greater advantage in the dimness. Candles and torches give too much light. Therefore lamps furnished with perfumed oil must be brought and the continual vapors from these lamps give sweetness and delight to the company. Now, these lamps give off a still more excellent fragrance and fill the room with a greater scent when they are extinguished. In many parts of Holy Scripture we find that lamps represent the saints. [*Sir.* 26:17; *Matt.* 5:16]. They are lamps which have given forth continual vapors of good examples before men and have always been burning fires of the love of God. Oh, what sweet perfumes these lamps gave forth before the Divine Majesty during the course of their lives, but especially at the hour of their death! The death of the just is precious in the eyes of the Lord [*Ps.* 116:15], while, on the contrary, the death of the wicked He holds in horror [*Ps.* 34:22] inasmuch as it carries them to damnation.

Now if the saints have been blazing and fragrant fires [*Song* 8:6; *Jn.* 5:35], how much more the most holy Virgin, whose perfection surpasses that of all the blessed? Even if all their perfections were united in one, they could not be comparable to hers. She was certainly a lamp fed with perfumed oil. What perfume do you think she gave forth at the hour of her glorious death? The maidens have gone after her, attracted by the odor of her perfumes. [*Song* 1:3-4]. The sacred soul of our glorious Mistress took flight directly to Heaven and went to give forth her perfumes before the Divine Majesty, who received her and placed her on a throne at the right hand of her Son.

But with what triumph, with what magnificence do you think she was welcomed by her Beloved Son in return for the love with which she had received Him when He came to earth? We must believe that He was not ungrateful, but that He rewarded her with a degree of glory as much above all the blessed spirits as her merits surpassed those of all the saints combined. The great Apostle St. Paul, in speaking of the glory of the Son of God Our Lord, makes use of an argument by which we may understand the high degree of glory of His most holy Mother. He says [*Heb.* 1:3-7] that Jesus Christ was raised as far superior to all the cherubim and other angelic spirits as the Name He has inherited is superior to all other names. It is written of the angels: You are My servants and My messengers; but to which of them was it said: "You are My Son; I have begotten You"?

We may speak in like manner of the most holy Virgin, who is the paragon of all that is beautiful in Heaven and on earth. To whom has it been said: "You are Mother of the Almighty and of the Son of God," except to her? Therefore, well may you think that she was exalted far above all that is not God.

When the most holy soul of Our Lady left her most pure body, this body was carried to the sepulcher and returned to the earth like that of her Son. For it was most proper that the Mother should not have a greater privilege than the Son. But just as Our Lord rose at the end of three days, so did she rise at the end of three days, yet in a different manner, inasmuch as the Saviour rose by His own power and authority and Our Lady rose by the almighty power of her Son, who commanded the blessed soul of His most holy Mother to be reunited to her body. Certainly it was very fitting that this most pure body should in no way be tainted by any corruption, since that of Our Lord had been drawn from her chaste womb and had reposed in it for nine months.

The Ark of the Covenant, in which were kept the Tables of the Law [*1 Kgs.* 8:9; *Heb.* 9:4], could not be attacked by any corruption because it was made of cedar wood,[3] which is incorruptible. [*Ex.* 25:10]. How much more reasonable that *this* "Ark"—in which had reposed the Master of the Law—should be exempt from all corruption. The resurrection of the most holy Virgin is declared by these words: Rise, Lord God, You and the ark of Your Majesty. [*2 Chr.* 6:41; *Ps.* 132:8]. As to the word "rise," it refers to the Resurrection of Our Lord; but those which follow, "and the ark of Your Majesty," must be understood of the resurrection of His Mother. As to our bodies, they are reduced to dust whether we will it or not, and this is the tribute which we owe and must all pay because of the sin we have all committed in Adam. "You are dirt and to dirt you shall return." [*Gen.* 3:19; *Eccl.* 12:7]. The maggots devour us, and we all have reason to say to the maggots: You are "my father"; you are "my mother." [*Job* 17:14].

I do not know whether you ever noticed that before undertaking the combat against Goliath, the little David inquired carefully among the soldiers what would be given to the person who conquered and overthrew that great giant, the enemy of the children of God. He was answered that the king had promised great riches to the one who would be so fortunate as to defeat him. But that was not enough for the heart of David, who was generous and thought nothing at all of riches. Honors were added to riches. Not only would the king enrich him, they said to David, but he would give him his daughter in marriage, he would make him his son-in-law, and, moreover, he even promised to exempt his house from tribute. [*1 Sam.* 17:25-27,30].

When Our Lord and Master came into this world, He inquired like His ancestor David what would be given to him who would conquer that powerful "Goliath," the devil, whom He Himself calls "the prince of this world" [*Jn.* 12:31; 14:30], because of the great power he had before the Incarnation of the Word. The same answer was given to Him as to David: The King will enrich the one who overcomes this cruel Goliath. And that this may be so, listen to what is said by the Eternal Father: I will appoint

him king and will give him full power over all that is in
Heaven and on earth. [*Ps.* 2:6-8; *Heb.* 1:2]. But Our Lord
would not have been satisfied if it had not been added that:
The King has promised that He will give him His daughter
in marriage.

Now the daughter of the King, that is to say of God, is
no other than glory. Our Divine Master was always most
glorious and always possessed all glory. As to the supreme
part of His soul, it was always united and joined inseparably to the Divinity from the moment of His Conception.
But the glory that was promised to Him was the glorifica-
tion of His body. Nevertheless, He would not even then
have been satisfied if it had not been added that His house
would be exempt from tribute. Now what is the house of
Our Lord if not the most holy and virginal flesh of Our
Lady? She was then exempt from tribute by the merits of
her Son. That is, she was raised up before she had received
any blemish or deterioration in the sepulcher.

What is there left for us to say now except to see
whether we can in some way imitate the Assumption of our
glorious and most worthy Mistress? As to our body, we
cannot imitate her until the day of the Last Judgment,
when the bodies of the blessed will rise glorious and those
of the reprobate will be damned forever. But as to her soul,
which went to be united and joined inseparably to the
Divine Majesty, let us see how we might imitate her in this.
It is said in the Gospel that Martha, into whose home Our
Lord entered, was anxious and hastened here and there to
treat Him well—while Mary seated herself at the Saviour's
feet, where she listened to His words. And while Martha
was taking care to nourish the body of her Master, Mary
relinquished all other care for the one care of nourishing
and sustaining her soul. This she did by listening to Our
Lord.

Martha was touched by a little twinge of envy. Extremely
few are free of it, however spiritual they may be. And the
more spiritual they are, so much the more subtle and im-

perceptible is the envy. It acts so dexterously that it is difficult to discover it. When we praise someone and reserve a little of the praise that we know is due, what prompts this if not our envy of his virtues? But Martha gives her little blow and casts her little dart of envy under cover of a pleasantry, and this is all the more subtle. Master, she said, are You allowing my sister not to help me, leaving me to do the household tasks all alone? Tell her to help me.

Our Lord is incomparably good; and although He well knew her imperfection, He did not reprove her severely, but most lovingly, for this Gospel is all love. The Evangelist notes that He called her by name, saying: Martha, Martha, you are anxious and upset about many things; one thing only is required. Mary has chosen the better portion and she shall not be deprived of it.

But let us say a few words on these little suggestions of envy that our self-love produces, which are certainly like little foxes that damage and destroy the vineyards. [*Song* 2:15]. Listen to religious when they speak of their Institute. They always esteem it above all others: "It is true," they say, "that the Order you speak of demands great perfection, but mine goes even further. Oh, I do not speak of myself but only of the great perfection to which they aspire in this house." Beware! For in the end you will turn back on yourself without even perceiving it. Another will say: "I am miserable and can do nothing of any value, but such a sermon as I preached . . .", and he will not hesitate to use these words when the preaching of another is praised. Thus when we hear someone praised, we say a little word in passing to attract attention to ourselves.

Let us return to Martha, who was so anxious. Certainly the rest of us can do nothing without anxiety, or, to speak more correctly, without using great care as to our exterior. We must know that there are two aspects in us which constitute only one person, the exterior and the interior. The interior always tends to union with the Divine Majesty and takes the necessary means to attain to this union. The exterior is whom we see, who looks, who speaks, who touches, who listens. It is he who is anxious in the exercise of the virtues which concern the commandment of love of the neighbor, while the interior practices the love of God. These two aspects thus exercise themselves in the observance of the two principal commandments upon which, as upon two pillars, are founded and fulfilled the whole Law and the prophets as well. [*Matt.* 22:40]. The ancient philosophers said that we must view the end before we begin the work. But we do just the contrary, for we are anxious in the performance of the work undertaken rather than in considering what must be its end.

Let us speak a little more clearly. The end of our life is death; therefore, we ought to think carefully of what our death should be and how we can achieve this so as to make our life correspond to the death we desire. For it is certain that as is our life, so will our death be; and as is our death, so has been our life.

Let us now examine how our exterior can do nothing, not even the practice of virtue, unaccompanied by extreme solicitude. The ancients who counted the virtues numbered a multitude of them, and in the end they still fell short. Let us enter upon this assessment of the virtues to see if we can learn to practice them without undue anxiety.

We must be very careful in the practice of modesty. Observe that person who intends to practice it. She begins by making an agreement with her eyes. [*Job* 31:1]. They shall only look at necessary things, nothing else. When not intended for flight, hawks are hooded in order to be carried more easily on the handle. She does the same to her eyes, for she draws over them their natural hood, which are the eyelids, that they may look at only what is necessary.[4] She also takes great care to practice continual modesty of demeanor, that she may not forget herself and yield to levity.

What attention is needed to practice patience and not give way to anger! Cassian writes that it is not sufficient to avoid the occasions of speaking and conversing with people. Avoiding its practice is not the means of acquiring the virtue. For he relates that, being alone in the desert, if he rose in the night and took his tinder box to light his candle and the flint did not strike fire, he flew into a passion and threw it onto the ground.[5]

Certainly we must be very careful not to yield to impatience, but, O my God! To be spiritually valiant, never to allow ourselves to be discouraged in doing good—this can only be accomplished by giving great attention to observing discretion. I say the same for constancy, perseverance, affability, prudence, temperance, and especially temperance in our words. What a bridle must we not put upon our tongue to prevent it from running through the streets like a runaway horse and entering into the house of the neighbor, even into his life, either to censure or control it, or to take from him a little of the esteem which we know is his due.

But, you will ask me, what is the remedy for avoiding so much solicitude, since I must exercise myself in virtue? Indeed this care is very praiseworthy, provided it is free of anxiety and eagerness. Nevertheless, I will give you a remedy which will free you from so much anxiety. Since Our Lord says that one thing only is required, which is to be saved, we are not required to multiply the means of advancing toward our salvation, although advancement is always necessary. I tell you in one word: Have most holy love and you will have all the virtues. That this is true, listen to the great Apostle: Love is gentle, it is patient, it is kind, it is condescending, it is humble, it is affable, there is no limit to its forebearance. [*1 Cor.* 13:4-7]. In short, it comprises in itself all the perfections of the other virtues, but much more excellently than they do themselves.[6] Love has but one single act, which is one of joining and union. To love God above all things is the first commandment; to love the neighbor above all that is not God is the reflection of the first commandment. [*Matt.* 22:37-39].

The most holy Virgin, our glorious Mistress, practiced

both these loves in the reception she gave to her Son. She loved Him and received Him as her God, and she received Him, loved Him and served Him as her neighbor. We cannot have one of these loves without the other. [*1 Jn.* 4:20-21]. Do you love God perfectly? Then you love the neighbor perfectly. In the measure that one of these loves increases, the other also increases. Likewise, if one diminishes, the other will soon grow less. If you have the love of God, do not be troubled or anxious about the exercise of the other virtues. For you will not fail to practice them when the opportunity presents itself. I say this of any virtue whatsoever: patience, meekness, modesty, and so of the rest.

Rabbits have little ones every three weeks. We find many leverets, flies by the thousands, countless gnats, but extremely few eagles. The elephant bears only one calf, the lioness never more than one lion.[7] Thus the exercise of Martha includes a number of acts, but that of Mary, which is love, has only one, which is, as we have said, that of joining and union.

It seems that, in a certain sense, the Assumption of Our Lady was more glorious and triumphant than the Ascension of Our Lord, because at the Ascension only the angels came to meet Him, but at the Assumption of His most holy Mother the King of Angels came Himself. Therefore, the angelic hosts exclaimed in astonishment: Who is this coming up from the desert, leaning on her Lover? [*Song* 8:5].

By this we may understand that although Our Lady ascended to Heaven as an all-pure being, yet notwithstanding her purity she was nevertheless leaning on the merits of her Son, in virtue of which she entered into glory. And just as there was never such an abundance of perfumes seen in the city of Jerusalem as the Queen of Sheba carried with her when she went to visit the great King Solomon, who in exchange made her presents according to his greatness and royal magnificence [*1 Kgs.* 10:1-2,10]; likewise, I say, never were there seen so many merits and so much love carried to Heaven by any pure creature as the most holy Virgin brought there at her glorious Assumption. In reward for this the eternal and great King, the Almighty God, gave her a degree of glory worthy of her greatness, and also power to distribute to her clients graces worthy of her liberality and magnificence. Amen.

NOTES

1. The passage does not in fact identify Martha's sister as Mary Magdalene, but only as Mary.
2. Cf. Sermon for August 15, 1602; St. Francis de Sales' *Treatise on the Love of God,* Book 7, Chapters 13 and 14. (In subsequent references this work will be referred to simply as *Treatise).*
3. Actually, Scripture speaks of acacia wood, rather than cedar wood— or, in the Douay version, of setim wood.
4. Cf. *Treatise,* Bk. 1, ch. 2.
5. Cf. *The Spiritual Conferences of St. Francis de Sales* (Westminster, Md.: Newman Press, 1962), III, "On Constancy," p.53; X, "On Obedience," p.166. (In subsequent references this work will be referred to simply as *Conferences.*)
6. Cf. *Treatise,* Bk. 11, ch. 8, 9.
7. Cf. *Treatise,* Bk. 10, ch. 7.

— 6 —

THE PRESENTATION OF OUR LADY IN THE TEMPLE

*Sermon for the Feast of the Presentation of Our
Lady, November 21, 1619, concerning Our Lady's
continual obedience to the will of God, her offering of herself to God in the Temple, the giving of
one's whole self to God through the religious
vows, regular renewal of good purposes and vows,
and total obedience to God's word.*

The Gospel proposed by Holy Church for today's feast
[*Lk.* 11:27 ff.] is composed of two parts, both of which
tend to the praise of the most holy Virgin whose Presentation in the Temple we are celebrating. The first part is
that, while Our Lord was preaching, a woman began to cry
out, speaking to Him in this manner: "Blest is the womb
that bore You and the breasts that nursed You!" To which
Our Lord replied: "Rather, blest are they who hear, who
pay attention to, the word of God and keep it!" I shall
dwell principally upon this latter because it is more to the
glory of the most sacred Virgin. Our Divine Master teaches
us this by His reply to this woman, for although the first
praise was inspired by the Holy Spirit Himself, it was
nevertheless pronounced by a creature. But since the
Saviour wished to enrich rather than diminish the praise
rendered His most holy Mother, He took up the canticle of
respect intoned by St. Marcella in honor of Our Lady, saying: "That is true, but happier indeed is she for having
paid attention to the word of My Father and having kept it.

Without doubt it is a very great honor to have borne Me in her womb and to have nourished Me with the milk from her breasts—I who am the Food of angels and men on high in heavenly glory. That, however, is not the foundation of her beatitude. Rather, to have been always obedient to the will of My Father is." Felicity is not attached to dignity, nor is it given in light of it, but according to the measure of union we have with the divine will. Thus, if we could separate the dignity of the Mother of God from the perfect submission which that most sacred Virgin had to His holy will, she would have the same degree of glory and the same felicity which she now has in Heaven. But I say this only in passing.

Our Lady had three great privileges above all pure creatures. The first is that she was always most obedient to the will of God, that is to say, to His word, and this from the very instant of her Conception, without any variation or interruption, not even for a single moment. She was never subject to change and could never sever this first union and adherence which she then made of her will to God's will. This favor was not accorded to any other pure creature, not even to the angels, for they could change and abandon the grace they had received from the Divine Majesty at their creation. Lucifer's fall and that of his followers shows this clearly. As for man, who can be a man and not know that he is inconstant and fickle? We ourselves experience this every day. Who is always of the same humor? Now we want one thing; soon we will have no more of it, but desire another. Now we are happy, then sad. In short, there is nothing but constant change.

Our Lady could never fall from the first grace which she received from the Sovereign Majesty because she always adhered to the divine will, so that she merited new graces without ceasing. The more she received of them, so much the more was her soul rendered capable of adhering to God, so that she was ever more united and rooted in her first union with Him. If we can find change in the most holy Virgin, it is only that of a closer union and further growth in all kinds of virtue in order to render invariable the resolution which she had made of belonging wholly to God. For this reason she wanted to withdraw to the Temple, not that she had need of it for herself, but in order to teach us that we, being subject to change, ought to use every possible means to strengthen and preserve our good resolutions, as much interiorly as exteriorly. As for her, in order to persevere in her good purpose it sufficed that she had given herself to God from the first moment of her life, without the need of leaving her father's home. She had nothing to fear, since exterior objects could never divert her. But like a good mother, she would teach us that we should neglect nothing to make permanent our calling, as St. Peter exhorts us. [*2 Pet.* 1:10].

The Holy Virgin had the use of reason from the instant of her Conception,[1] and from that same instant the Divine Goodness preserved her from the precipice of Original Sin into which she would have fallen had not His all-powerful hand prevented her. In thanksgiving for this grace she dedicated and consecrated herself to His service so absolutely from that time that the promise she made to the Divine Majesty was irrevocable. But notwithstanding that, for the space of three years she kept her resolution sealed and hidden under the appearance of infancy. I say "under the appearance of infancy" because in reality she was not an infant at all. Since she had the use of reason she led a purely contemplative life. She was so wise a child that we can never imagine another such, except her well-beloved Son. When three, she was carried part of the way from Nazareth to Jerusalem, but the rest of the distance she went with her own little steps. Pious tradition reports that it was a charming picture to see how joyously she mounted the 15 steps of the Temple.

We are now at the second part of our discourse. St. Joachim and St. Anne brought her in order to fulfill a vow they had made to God to offer her in His Temple. But this blest child came there motivated also by her own will. To keep herself in the bounds of infancy she had indeed not manifested this. Nevertheless, she had long waited to see herself absolutely and wholly consecrated to the Divine Majesty. With an unparalleled heart she came to give herself to God without reserve; and had she dared to speak, no doubt she would have said to the good women who brought up those maidens who were dedicated to Our Lord in the Temple: "I am here in your hands like a ball of wax. Do with me what you will, I shall make no resistance." Moreover, she was so pliable and submissive that she allowed herself to be turned by every hand without ever testifying any desire for this or that, so condescending that all were overcome with admiration.

From that time she began to imitate her Son, who was to be totally submissive to the will of all. Though indeed it was in His power to resist all, still He would never do so. At the beginning of His Passion He manifested His omnipotence when, as the Lion of the tribe of Juda [*Rev.* 5:5], He roared out: "I am He." When He asked the Jews who were seeking Him: "Who is it you want?" they answered Him: "Jesus, the Nazorean." "I am He," He said; and by this word He threw all His enemies to the ground. [*Jn.* 18:4-6]. But immediately upon raising them up, He again concealed His omnipotence under the mantle of a holy gentleness and meekness. And from the moment they laid hold of Him until they led Him to death they never again saw in Him any resistance whatsoever. He even permitted them not only to shear Him as a trusting lamb [*Is.* 53:7; *Jer.* 12:19], but also to deprive Him of His very skin. The sacred Virgin foresaw all this and submitted herself without any reserve, giving and abandoning herself wholly to the mercy of the divine will.

This is the second privilege which she had above all creatures, for no one ever gave himself so perfectly and so absolutely to the Divine Majesty as she did. She was more perfectly obedient to the word of God than any other creature. Moreover, she was more submissive than anyone else ever was. Who gives all reserves nothing. But what, I ask you, is it to give all to God? It is not to reserve for oneself anything which may not be for God, not even a single one of our affections or our desires. And what does God ask of us? Listen, I beg you, to this sacred Saviour of our souls: My son, give Me your heart. [*Prov.* 23:26]. He keeps repeating this to each one of us.

But, you will ask me, how can I give God my heart, so full of sins and imperfections? How could it be pleasing to Him, since it is filled with disobedience to His wishes? Alas, poor man, why afflict yourself so? Why do you refuse to give it to Him such as it is? Do you not know that He did not say: "Give Me a pure heart like that of the angels or of Our Lady," but: "Give Me your heart"? He asks for your own heart. Give it such as it is. For, ah! Are we not aware that everything that is remitted into His divine hands is converted into good? [Cf. *Rom.* 8:28]. Is your heart of the earth, vile and filled with filth? Still do not fear to remit it into the hands of God. When God created Adam, He took a little clay from the ground and then made of it a living being. [*Gen.* 2:7]. Is your heart well disposed? Give it, such as it is, for that is what the Divine Goodness asks. He desires only what we are and what we have.

In the Old Law God ordained that everyone should visit His Temple, but He forbade anyone, either poor or rich, to come there empty-handed [*Ex.* 23:15; *Dt.* 16:16]. Moreover, He did not wish that all should make an equal offering; for He wished that the rich, the affluent, should offer according to their riches, and the poor, according to their poverty. [*Lev.* 12:8; *Dt.* 16:17; *Lk.* 2:24]. He was not satisfied if a rich man made an offering suitable to the poor, because that manifested avarice; nor if a poor man made the offering of the rich, for that would be presumption. When the laity come to offer to the Divine Majesty their affections and the will they have to follow His commandments, God will be pleased with them and they will be very happy. For if they observe these commandments faithfully, they will be saved. [*Matt.* 19:17]. But souls who are rich in holy aspirations to do great things for God should not come bringing the offering of the poor. For God will not be pleased with it. The Lord has enriched you with His grace and He wants you to bring Him what you have.

Today Our Lady makes an offering such as God desires. Besides the dignity of her person, which surpasses that of all others after her Son, she offers all that she is and all that she has, and that is what God asks. Oh, how happy are we who, by means of the vows which we have made, have dedicated ourselves wholly to Him: our bodies, our hearts, and our goods. We renounce riches by the vow of poverty, the pleasures of the flesh by the vow of chastity, and our own will by the vow of obedience. O people of the world, enjoy your goods if you wish, provided you wrong no one. Take the lawful pleasures permitted you by Holy Church. Do your own will in such and such occurrences. God allows you all that. But as for us, let us take care to reserve nothing, for God does not want any reserve. He wants all. As He gives Himself wholly to us in His Divine Sacrament, so does He want us quite entirely. Take care, for no one makes a fool of God. [*Gal.* 6:7]. If we say that we are resolved to give all, let us do so absolutely, under pain of being chastised like Ananias and his wife Saphira, who lied to the Holy Spirit. [*Acts* 5:1-10].

But it is not with us as it was with Our Lady. Having once given herself to God, she had no need of again confirming her offering. For not even for a single moment did she ever cease belonging wholly to God and being attached to and united with His divine will. We, on the contrary, because of the continual vicissitudes of life and the inconstancy of our affections and humors, must every hour, every day, every month, and every year confirm again and renew the vows and promises we made to be all God's. That is why, not only in the New Law but in the Old as well, they always made it a point of setting aside certain seasons and certain days in order to encourage the people to renew their good resolutions.

The Israelites were the people of God. They made their renewal at each new moon, and in order to attract everyone they celebrated solemn feasts. They sounded trumpets [*Lev.* 23:24; *Num.* 10:10; 29:1; *Ps.* 81:4] in order to rouse the spirit, not to fanfare or vain things, but for the things of eternity. And Holy Church, like a wise mother, from time to time throughout the year gives us special feasts in order to encourage us to renew our good purposes. On the solemn day of Easter, for instance, who does not renew himself totally by his holy affections and resolutions to do better, seeing Our Lord wholly renewed in His Resurrection? Who is the Christian who does not renew his heart on the day of Pentecost, when he considers how God sends from Heaven a new spirit upon those who love Him [*Ps.* 51:12; *Ezech.* 18:31; *Acts* 2:17], and on All Saints Day, when Holy Church represents to us the glory and felicity of the blessed, for which we long and in which we hope? Finally, who can have so little courage as not to undergo a renewal of spirit on Christmas Day when he sees the Saviour of our souls become so lovable a baby, coming to ransom us?

But besides all these feasts, it has been the custom of all those who have more especially dedicated themselves to God, such as religious, to take a particular day for renewing their vows in order the better to obey the great Apostle St. Peter who counsels us to make permanent our calling.[2] [*2 Pet.* 1:10]. And how could we better do this than by again confirming our intention and the choice which we have made? Thus today, my dear Sisters, you have strengthened your vocation by renewing your vows in the presence of the Divine Majesty. He asks that of you in acknowledgement of the sacred gift He made to you at the same time—the gift of Himself.

I cannot develop the third privilege of the glorious Virgin. Let us say, however, that she was obedient to the

Divine Majesty, not only to His commandments but also to
His desires and good pleasure and to His inspirations. In
that, my dear Sisters, we must take care to imitate her as
closely as possible. I say this because very few are found
who do it faithfully, though many protest that they are
resolved to do so. To obey the will of God is to obey His
word. Ask any Christian if he is not resolved to obey God's
word. "Oh, without doubt I am." But listen to Our Lord,
who says: How blest are the poor in spirit. [*Matt.* 5:3, 5].
Yet, there are few indeed who do not desire to be rich! "As
for me, I do not care to be rich at all. I love poverty." Yes,
provided nothing is wanting to you.

And this word of the Saviour: Happy the gentle. And
who takes account of this? I come from the world and I
can assure you there are very few to be found who practice
it. When we preach gentleness to them in light of what Our
Lord has said: Learn from Me, for I am gentle and humble
of heart [*Matt.* 11:29], there are few who do not reply: But
those who are gentle do not make themselves feared
enough. Ah, if you want to be feared you will not be humble, for there is nothing more contrary to humility. Note
that our Divine Master desired to be feared only once in
His life, upon which I have already touched.[3] That is,
when He said to those who wished to seize Him in the
Garden of Olives: "I am He." There are fewer still who
would put faith in *this* word: Blest are those persecuted for
holiness' sake. [*Matt.* 5:10].

There is no more exception from this obedience than
from the offering of ourselves that God wishes us to make
Him. For if Our Lady would not have been pleasing to the
Divine Majesty without this absolute obedience, as Our
Lord showed by the praise He gave her after that of that
holy woman mentioned in our Gospel, how much less
pleasing would we be? Besides, my dear Sisters, although
no other than the Holy Virgin could have had this honor of
being Mother of Our Lord in reality, we ought nevertheless
to strive to merit the name of it by obedience to the will of

God. You know that one day when the Saviour was preaching the words of eternal life [*Jn.* 6:68] in the Temple, Our Lady was at the door and someone came to say that His Mother and His brothers were seeking Him (for there were some of His relatives whom He called His "brothers"). He replied: Who is My mother? Who are My brothers? They who do the will of My Heavenly Father....[4] [*Matt.* 12:46-50].

NOTES

1. In describing Our Lady's great privileges and favors St. Francis de Sales is always careful to point out that they are the results of God's grace on her behalf. It is worth noting that the editor of the Annecy edition indicates that these lines, and others in this sermon, are not edited in the original manuscript.
2. Cf. above, p. 76-77.
3. Cf. above, p. 78.
4. This sermon ends somewhat abruptly.

7

THE PURIFICATION
OF THE BLESSED VIRGIN MARY

*Sermon for the Feast of the Purification, February
2, 1620, concerning the voluntary subjection of
Our Lord and His Blessed Mother to the laws of
presentation and purification, their practice of
humility, various sins of pride, the perfect obedience of Our Lord and His Mother, how we
should practice humility and obedience, and the
four conditions for praying well, in imitation of
the prophet Simeon who held the Divine Infant in
his arms.*

God speaks as He acts and acts as He speaks. [*Ps.* 33:9;
148:5]. In this He shows us that we must not be satisfied
with speaking well, but we must adjust our deeds to our
proposals and our works to our words if we want to be
pleasing to Him.

With God every word is act. He desires that, in the same
way, our words should be immediately followed by action
and the carrying out of our good resolutions. When the ancients would represent a man of integrity they used as a
symbol a peach upon which they laid a peach leaf, because
the peach has the form of a heart and the leaf of the peach
the form of a tongue. This signifies that the man of integrity and virtue has not only a tongue in order to say
many good things, but that since this tongue is laid upon
his heart, he speaks only according to the wishes of his
heart. That is to say, he says only those words which first

spring from his heart, which immediately urges him to the accomplishment and effects of his words. For the same reason the four animals had not only wings with which to fly, but also hands under them [*Ezech.* 1:5-8] to help us understand that we ought not to be satisfied in having wings in order to fly to Heaven by holy desires and considerations, if, along with these, we have not also hands which lead us to works and the execution of our desires. It is certain that good desires and holy resolutions alone will not take us to Paradise unless they are accompanied by effects conformable to them.

To confirm this truth Our Lord comes to the Temple today to be offered to God His Father, subjecting Himself to the observance of the Law which He had formerly given to Moses, written on stone tablets. [*Ex.* 24:12; 34:1; *2 Cor.* 3:7]. In this Law there was a great number of particular observances to which our Divine Master and Our Lady were in no way obliged. Being King and Monarch of the whole earth, indeed of Heaven, of earth, and of all that they contain, the Saviour could not be subject to any law or commandment. Nevertheless, because He was to be placed before our eyes as a sovereign and incomparable model to which we ought to conform ourselves in all things insofar as the weakness of our nature would permit, He chose to observe the Law and to subject Himself to it. His most blessed Mother followed His example, as we see in the Gospel of today [*Lk.* 2:22-38], which proposes to us the Purification of Our Lady and the Presentation of Our Lord in the Temple.

On this subject I will make three considerations, which I will not dwell upon but only touch on in passing, leaving them for you to ruminate in your mind, as "clean animals" [*Lev.* 11:2-3,47] do, to make a good and healthy digestion. The first consideration is on the example that our Divine Saviour and the glorious Virgin give us of a profound and true humility; the second, on obedience which is engrafted on humility; and the third, on the excellent method that they teach us for praying well.

First, what greater and more profound humility could be imagined than that which Our Lord and Our Lady practice in coming to the Temple: The One comes to be offered there the same as other children of sinful men, while the other comes to be purified! It is certain that Our Lord could not be obliged to this ceremony, since He was purity itself, and it referred only to sinners. As to Our Lady, what need had she to be purified? She neither was nor could be blemished, having received so excellent a grace from the time of her Conception that the cherubim's and seraphim's is in no way comparable to it. For if indeed God prevented[1] them with His grace from their creation to forestall their falling into sin, nevertheless they were not confirmed in grace from that moment in such a way that they could no longer deviate from it. But they were so afterwards, in virtue of the choice they made to avail themselves of this first grace and by the voluntary submission of their free will. But Our Lady was prevented with the grace of God and confirmed in it at the very moment of her Conception in such a way that she could not deviate from it nor sin. Nevertheless both the Child and the Mother, notwithstanding their incomparable purity, come today to present themselves in the Temple as if they were sinners like the rest of men. O act of incomparable humility!

The greater the dignity of the persons who humble themselves, the more estimable is the act of humility they make. O God! How great are Our Lord and Our Lady who is His Mother! What a beautiful consideration, the most useful and profitable that could be made, is that of the humility that the Saviour so dearly loved! It seems that it was His beloved, and that He descended from Heaven to earth only for the love of it.[2] [Lk. 1:48]. It is the greatest of all the purely moral virtues, for I am not speaking here of the love of God and of charity. Charity is not only a particular virtue but also a general one, which permeates all the others, and they receive their splendor from it. But as to particular virtues, there is none so great nor so necessary as humility. Our Lord so cherished humility that He preferred to die rather than abandon its practice. He Himself said: "There is no greater love than this: to lay down one's life" for the thing loved. [*Jn.* 15:13]. Now He truly gave His life for this virtue, for in dying He made the most excellent and most supreme act of humility that could ever be imagined. The Apostle St. Paul, to make us conceive in some degree the love our Saviour had for this holy virtue, says that "he humbled himself, obediently accepting even death, death on a cross" [*Phil.* 2:8], as if to say: My Master did not humble Himself for a time only or for some particular actions, but *to death,* that is to say, from the moment of His conception, and then during the whole course of His life, to death; and not only until then, but He willed to practice it even in dying. And enhancing the greatness of this humility, the Apostle adds: "even death on a cross"—a death more ignominious and full of abjection than any other kind of death.

By this divine example we are taught that we must not be satisfied with practicing humility in some particular actions or for a time only, but always and on every occasion; not only to death, but to the mortification of ourselves. In this way we humble the love of our own esteem and the esteem of our self-love. We must not amuse ourselves with the practice of a certain humility of demeanor and words which consists in saying that we are nothing and in making many exterior reverences and humiliations, which are anything but true humility. For humility, in order to be true, should not only make us know but also acknowledge that we are true nothings who do not deserve to live. It makes us docile, tractable and submissive to everyone, observing by this means that precept of the Saviour which orders us to renounce ourselves if we would follow Him. [*Matt.* 16:24].

There are some who greatly deceive themselves in thinking that the practice of humility is proper only to novices and beginners, and that as soon as they have made a little progress in the way of God they can easily relax in this practice. In fact, esteeming themselves already sufficiently wise, they turn into fools instead. [*Rom.* 1:22]. Do they not see that Our Lord humbled Himself even to death, that is to say, during the whole course of His life? Oh, how this Divine Master of our souls knew well that His example was necessary for us! He had no need of abasing Himself. Nevertheless He desired to persevere in doing this because the necessity was in us! Oh, how extremely necessary is perseverance in this matter, for how many have there been who, having begun very well in the practice of humility, have been lost through lack of perseverance. Our Lord did not say: "He who begins," but "he who holds out till the end" in humility will escape death. [*Matt.* 10:22; 24:13].

What made the angels sin except a lack of humility? Although their sin was one of disobedience, nevertheless to consider it in its origin it was pride which made them disobey. The miserable Lucifer began to look at and contemplate himself. Then he went on to admire and delight in his beauty, after which he said: "I will not serve," and thus he threw off the yoke of holy submission. [*Is.* 14:13-14; *Jer.* 2:20]. He had good reason to look at himself and consider his excellent nature, but not to delight in it and take empty pride in it. There is no evil at all in considering oneself in order to glorify God for the gifts that He has given us, provided that we do not pass on to vanity and self-complacency. There is a maxim of the philosophers which has been approved as good by Christian Doctors: "Know thyself"—that is to say, know the excellence of your soul in order not to disparage nor despise it. However, we must always remain within the terms and limits of a holy and loving acknowledgment before God, on whom we depend and who made us what we are. [*Ps.* 100:3].

Our first parents and all others who have sinned have almost all been moved to do so through pride. Our Lord, as a good and loving Doctor of our souls, takes evil in its root, and in place of pride He plants first the beautiful and useful plant of most holy humility. This virtue is so much the more necessary as its contrary vice is more general among all people. We have seen how pride was found among the angels and how the lack of humility was the reason for their being lost forever. See how, among men, some, having begun well, are miserably lost through lack of perseverance in this virtue. What did not King Saul do at the beginning of his reign? Scripture says that he had the innocence of a child of one year.[3] However, he was perverted to such a degree through his pride that he merited to be condemned by God. What humility did not Judas evince while living in the company of Our Lord? And yet see what pride he had when dying. Being unwilling to humble himself and perform the acts of penitence, which presuppose a very great and true humility, he despaired of obtaining pardon. [*Matt.* 27:4-5]. It is an insupportable pride to be unwilling to abase oneself before the Divine Mercy, from which we ought to expect all our good and all our happiness.

In short, this is the evil common among all people. That is why we can never preach enough and impress upon their minds the necessity of perseverance in the practice of the most holy and most lovable virtue of humility. For this purpose Our Lord and Our Lady come today to take upon themselves the mark of sinners—they who could not sin. They subject themselves to the Law which was made neither for the One nor the other. Great humility to abase oneself thus!

The humility practiced by little people is no great thing, nor is it an abasement of much importance in comparison with that of giants. Cats, rats and other such animals which almost crawl on the earth have no great difficulty in rising again when they have fallen or dropped to the ground. But elephants, once they have lowered themselves or fallen, have very great trouble and difficulty in rising and getting back on their feet. Likewise, it is no great thing to see us

abase and humble ourselves—the likes of us who are only
nothings and deserve only abjection and humiliation. But
the humiliations of our dear Saviour and the sacred Virgin,
who are like giants of incomparable magnificence and emi-
nence, are of inestimable value. From the moment they first
humbled themselves they persevered during the whole
course of their lives and never desired to rise again; for
Our Lord—and His most blessed Mother in imitation of
Him—"humbled himself, obediently accepting even death,
death on a cross."⁴ [*Phil.* 2:8]. But the likes of us miserable
creatures who, like rats, cats and other such animals, only
crawl and drag ourselves along the ground, as soon as we
have abased and humbled ourselves in some trifling cir-
cumstance, immediately rise up again, become haughty,
and seek to be esteemed something good.

We are impurity itself and we desire that others believe
us to be pure and holy. Great folly—greater indeed than
can be expressed! Our Lady, who never sinned, nevertheless was willing to be accounted a sinner. Consider, please,
a daughter of Eve: how ambitious she is for honor and to
be esteemed. Indeed, although this evil is general among
men, it nevertheless seems that this sex is more inclined to
it than the other.⁵ Our glorious Mistress was by no means a
daughter of Eve according to the spirit, but only according
to blood. For she was never anything but extremely humble
and lowly, as she herself says in her sacred canticle: The
Lord has looked upon His servant in her lowliness. That is
why all nations shall call me blessed. [*Lk.* 1:48].

I know well that she meant that God had looked upon
her littleness and her lowliness,⁶ but it is precisely in this
that we recognize still more her profound and sincere
humility. Listen to her, please, as she always depreciates
herself, and particularly when the angel announces to her
that she is to be the Mother of the Son of God: I am, she
says, His servant. [*Lk.* 1:38]. Therefore, to conclude this
first point (for we must be brief since this subject comes up
so often), we are taught by our Divine Master of the

esteem that we ought to have for most holy humility, which has always been His "well-beloved."[7] Moreover, it is the basis and foundation of the whole edifice of our perfection. This can neither stand nor be raised higher except by means of the practice of a profound, sincere and true acknowledgment of our littleness and stupidity. This practice leads us to a true humiliation and contempt of ourselves.[8]

Let us go on to the second point. The humility of our Divine Saviour and His most blessed Mother was always accompanied by a perfect obedience. Obedience had such power over both of them that they would rather have died, and even by death on a cross, than fail to obey. Our Lord died on the Cross through obedience. And Our Lady— what remarkable acts of obedience did she not make at the very hour of the death of her Son, who was the Heart of her heart? In no way whatever did she resist the will of the Heavenly Father, but rather remained firm and constant at the foot of the Cross [*Jn.* 19:25], completely submissive to the divine good pleasure. We can use the same words of St. Paul for obedience as we have for humility: Our Lord became obedient to death, even to death on a Cross.[9] [*Phil.* 2:8]. He never did anything throughout His entire life except through obedience, which He Himself made known to us when He said: It is not to do My own will that I have come down from Heaven, but to do the will of Him who sent Me. [*Jn.* 6:38]. Therefore, always and in all things He looked to the will of His Heavenly Father in order to follow it, and not for a time, but always and even unto death.

As to Our Lady, examine and consider the whole course of her life. You will find there nothing but obedience. She so esteemed this virtue that, although she had made a vow of virginity, she nevertheless submitted herself to the command that was given her to marry. Ever afterwards she persevered in obedience, as we see today, since she comes to the Temple to obey the law of purification, even though there was no necessity for her to observe it, nor her Son either, as we have already mentioned in the first point. Her obedience was purely voluntary. It was not less for being voluntary and unnecessary. She so dearly loved this virtue, which her sacred Son had engrafted as a divine graft on the trunk of holy humility, that she recommended no other. We do not find in the Gospel that she spoke except at the marriage feast of Cana in Galilee, when she said: Do whatever my Son tells you [*Jn.* 2:5], thus preaching the observance of obedience. This virtue is the inseparable companion of humility. One is never found without the other, for humility makes us submit to obedience.

Our Lady and sacred Mistress was not afraid of disobeying, because she was in no way obliged to the Law, which was not made for her or for her Son. Rather, she feared the shadow of disobedience. For though she, being all pure, had no need of being purified, if she had not come to the Temple to offer Our Lord and to be purified, there could have been found those who would wish to investigate her life in order to find out why she had not done as the rest of women. Thus she comes today to the Temple to remove all suspicion from men who might have wondered about her. She comes also to show us that we ought not to be satisfied with avoiding sin, but that we must avoid even the shadow of sin. Neither must we stop at the resolution we make not to commit such and such a sin; rather, we must fly even from the occasions which could serve as a temptation to fall into it. She also teaches us not to be satisfied with the testimony of a good conscience, but to take care to remove every suspicion in others that will make them disedified by us or by our conduct. I say this for certain people who, being resolved not to commit some sins, are not careful enough to avoid the suggestion they give that they would willingly commit them if they dared.

Oh, how this example of most holy obedience that Our Lord and Our Lady give us should incite us to submit ourselves absolutely and without any reserve to the observance of all that is commanded us, and, not satisfied with that, to observe also the things which are counseled in order to make us more pleasing to the Divine Goodness! My God! Is it such a great thing to see us obey, we who are born only to serve, since the Supreme King to whom all things should be subject [*Ps.* 119:91] was pleased to subject Himself to obedience? Let us then meditate on this sacred example that the Saviour and the glorious Virgin give us, and learn to submit ourselves—to make ourselves docile, pliable and easy to turn in any direction through most holy obedience; and not for a time nor for certain particular acts, but always, during the whole course of our life, even unto death.

In the third place let us consider in today's Gospel how we can observe an excellent way to pray well. Many greatly deceive themselves, believing that so many things are necessary, so many methods needed to pray well. We see some who are very anxious to research all possible means of finding a certain skill that to them seems necessary in order to know how to pray well. They ceaselessly analyze their prayer minutely, prying into it to see if they can make it as they desire. Some think they must not cough or stir for fear God's Spirit will withdraw—very great folly indeed, as if God's Spirit were so delicate that He depended on the method or the countenance of those who pray! I am not saying that we must not use methods which are taught. But we ought not to attach ourselves to them. Nor ought we to esteem them so much that we place all our confidence in them, as do those who think that provided they always make their considerations before the affections, all is well. It is very good to make considerations, but it is not good to attach oneself so much to one method or another that we think that all depends on our effort.

There is only one thing necessary to pray well, and that is to have Our Lord in our arms. When we do this our prayer is always made well, whatever method we follow. There is no other technique, and without this our prayers will be worth nothing—nor will God receive them. For the Divine Master has Himself said: No one comes to the Father except through Me. [*Jn.* 14:6]. Prayer is nothing else but an "elevation of our mind to God,"[10] which we in no way can bring about by ourselves. But when we have our Saviour in our arms everything becomes easy for us. Consider, please, the holy man Simeon and how well he prayed when he had Our Lord in his arms. "Now," he said, "You can let Your servant go in peace," since he has seen his salvation and his God. [*Lk.* 2:29-30]. It would be a horrible wickedness to wish to exclude Our Lord Jesus Christ from our prayer and to think that we could make it well without His assistance, for it is a sure fact that we cannot be pleasing to the Eternal Father except when He regards us through His Son, our Saviour [*Ps.* 84:10; *Rom.* 8:29]. And this is true not only of men but also of angels, for although He is not their Redeemer, He is nevertheless their Saviour, and they have been confirmed in grace by Him. Just as when we look at something through a red or violet glass everything we see is of that color, so the Eternal Father, looking at us through the beauty and goodness of His most blessed Son, finds us beautiful and good as He desires us to be. But without this artifice we are only ugliness and deformity itself.[11]

I have said that prayer is "an elevation to God." It is true, for although in going to God we meet the angels or the saints on our way, we do not raise our mind to them nor do we address our prayers to them, as the heretics have unfairly suggested. We simply ask them to join their prayers to ours in order to make of them a holy fusion, so that by this sacred mingling ours might be better received by the Divine Goodness. God always finds them agreeable if we bring along with us His dear Benjamin, as the children of Jacob did when they went to see their brother Joseph in Egypt. [*Gen.* 43:15]. If we do not take Him with us, we will receive the same punishment with which Joseph threatened his brothers, that is, that never again would they be admitted to his presence, and they would receive nothing from him, if they did not bring their little brother to him. [*Gen.* 42:20; 43:3].

Our dear little brother is this blessed Baby that Our Lady carries to the Temple today and whom she hands over—either she personally or through St. Joseph—to the good old man Simeon. It is more likely that it was St. Joseph rather than the sacred Virgin. There are two reasons for this. First, it was the fathers who came to offer their children, having a greater role here than even the mothers. The other reason is that women were not yet purified and dared not approach the altar where the offerings were made. [*Lev.* 12:4]. However that may be, it does not matter much. It is enough that St. Simeon received this very blessed Baby into his arms, either from Our Lady or St. Joseph. Oh, how happy are they who go to the Temple ready to receive the grace of receiving from this divine Mother—or from her dear spouse—Our Lord and Master! Having Him in our arms we desire nothing more and can well sing this divine canticle: Now You can dismiss Your servant in peace, O my God, because my soul is fully satisfied, possessing all that is most desirable either in Heaven or on earth. [*Ps.* 73:25].

But please consider a little the conditions necessary for obtaining this favor of taking the Saviour in our arms and of receiving Him from the hands of Our Lady as did St. Simeon and Anna, that good widow who had the happiness of being in the Temple at this very moment. The Church has us sing that St. Simeon was just and God-fearing. [*Lk.* 2:25]. In many places in Holy Scripture this word "fearing" means reverence for God and the things of His service. Thus he was full of reverence for sacred things. Moreover, he awaited the Redemption of Israel, "and the Holy Spirit was upon him." [*Lk.* 2:25]. These are the four conditions necessary in order to pray well, for we must first have them before we can hold Our Lord in our arms, in which true prayer consists.

First, Simeon was just. What does this mean but that he had adjusted[12] his will to God's? To be just is nothing else than to exist according to the Heart of God and to live according to His good pleasure. As for the rest of us, we are that much less capable of praying to the extent that our will is not united and adjusted to that of Our Lord.

I want to make myself better understood. Ask a person where she is going; [she answers:] "I am going to pray." That is good. May God grant you the accomplishment of your desire and undertaking! But tell me, please, what are you going to do in prayer? "I am going to ask God for consolations." You have expressed yourself well. You do not, then, wish to adjust your will to the will of God, who wishes that you should have dryness and sterility? That is not being just. "Oh! I am going to ask God to deliver me from so many distractions which come and bother me at prayer." Alas! Do you not see that all of that preoccupation renders your will incapable of being united and adjusted to that of Our Lord, who desires that, on entering prayer, you should be resolved to bear the pain of continual distractions, dryness, and disgusts which will befall you there? He wants you to remain as content with these as if you had many consolations and great tranquility. For it is certain that your prayer will not be less pleasing to God nor less useful to you for having been made with many difficulties. So long as we adjust our will to that of the Divine Majesty in all events, whether in prayer or in any other matter, our prayers and everything else will be both useful to us and pleasing in the eyes of His Goodness.

The second condition which we find necessary for praying well is that of awaiting, as did the good St. Simeon, the Redemption of Israel—that is to say, that we live in expectation of our own perfection. Oh, how happy are they who, living in expectation, do not grow weary of waiting! I say this for the sake of some who, desiring perfection by the acquisition of virtues, wish to have them at once, as if perfection consisted only in desiring it. It certainly would be a great good if we could be humble as soon as we had the desire to be so, without any trouble. Again, suppose an angel could one day fill a sacristy with virtues and with perfection itself, and we would only have to go there and clothe ourselves with it as we would with a garment. Certainly, this would be wonderful. But this being impossible, we must get used to seeking the attainment of our perfection by the ordinary ways, in tranquility of heart. We must do all that we can to acquire virtues by our fidelity in practicing them, each of us according to our condition and vocation. And let us remain in expectation regarding the attainment, sooner or later, of our goal, leaving that to Divine Providence, who will take care to console us, as He did St. Simeon, at the time He has destined to do so. [*1 Pet.* 5:7,10]. And even if this should be only at the hour of our death, that ought to be enough for us, provided that we fulfill our duty by always doing what lies in our power to do. We will always have soon enough what we desire when we have it when it pleases God to give it to us.

The third condition is that, like St. Simeon, we must be God-fearing—that is, full of reverence before God at the time of holy prayer. For how full of respect and reverence should we not be when speaking to the Divine Majesty, since the angels who are so pure tremble in His presence? "But my God! [You may answer:] I am not able to have this consciousness of the presence of God which causes so great a humiliation in my whole soul, that is, in all the faculties of my soul—in short, that sensible reverence which would make me annihilate myself so sweetly and agreeably before God." It is not of this I mean to speak, but rather of that which keeps the supreme part and point of our spirit low and in humility before God in acknowledgment of His infinite greatness and our profound littleness and unworthiness. Oh! How good it is to see the respect with which this holy man Simeon holds the Divine Infant in his arms, since he knows the sovereign dignity of Him whom he holds!

In the fourth place, it is said that the Holy Spirit was upon St. Simeon and that He made His dwelling in him. It was for that reason that he deserved to see Our Lord and to hold Him in his arms. Thus it is necessary for us to make room within ourselves for the Holy Spirit if we wish Our Lady or St. Joseph to let us hold and carry in our arms this Divine Saviour of our souls. All our happiness consists in this since we can approach His Heavenly Father only through His mediation and His favor. [*Rom.* 5:2; *Eph.* 2:18; 3:12]. Now what must we do to make room within ourselves for the Holy Spirit? "The Spirit of the Lord fills the world." [*Wis.* 1:7]. Yet, it is said in another place that He does not dwell in a cunning and deceitful heart. [*Wis.* 1:4-5]. It is a wonderful thing that this Divine Spirit does not hesitate to dwell in us, except for those who are cunning and deceitful! Therefore we must be simple and ingenuous if we wish the Holy Spirit to come into us, and Our Lord after Him. The Holy Spirit seems to be the harbinger of our Saviour Jesus Christ, for just as He proceeds from Him from all eternity as God, it seems that the roles are reversed now, Our Lord proceeding from *Him* as man.[13]

What more shall we now say except that having the Holy Spirit in us during this perishable and mortal life, holding ourselves in great respect and reverence before the Divine Majesty while awaiting with submission the attainment of our perfection, and, as far as possible, adjusting our will to that of God, we will have the happiness of carrying the Saviour in our arms and being blessed eternally by this grace. Amen.

NOTES

1. Preventing grace: the grace that goes before the free consent of the will. It moves the will spontaneously, inclining it to God.
2. Cf. Sermon for July 2, 1618, p. 54-55.

3. *1 Kgs.* 13:1, *Douay:* "Saul was a child of one year when he began to reign...." Douay footnote: "of one year—that is, he was good and like an innocent child."
4. Cf. above, p. 87.
5. Keep in mind that St. Francis' congregation here is a community of nuns.
6. Cf. Sermon for July 2, 1618, p. 53-55.
7. The French reads "sa bien cherie," an expression of endearment difficult to render into English.
8. St. Francis is strong on this point. Humility is the foot-rest of God's mercy toward us as well as the foundation for genuine and lasting growth in holiness.
9. Cf. above, p. 87.
10. Cf. vol. 1 of this series, *The Sermons of St. Francis de Sales on Prayer,* p. 5.
11. This language, though similar in tone to Luther's imputation language, underlines the mediatorial role of Christ, as the Biblical references, *Ps.* 84:10 and *Rom.* 8:29, make clear.
12. The pun is also present in the original French. Cf. *Conferences,* XIX, p. 382.
13. Although the structure is a bit awkward here, St. Francis de Sales is giving expression to this truth: Within the Trinity, the Father begets the Son and together they spirate the Holy Spirit. In the economy of salvation, the opposite movement takes place. We go to the Father through the Son in the Holy Spirit, the Spirit leading us to Jesus who, in turn, is the way to the Father.

8

THE NATIVITY
OF THE BLESSED VIRGIN MARY

*Sermon during the octave of the Feast of the birth
of the Blessed Virgin, September 10, 1620,
regarding renunciation of the world, the flesh and
self-will; Mary as "captainess" of the female sex
in the warfare of renunciation, Mary as model of
complete renunciation in the religious life, the
perfect renunciation practiced by Our Lady from
her infancy, and the renunciation practiced by St.
Nicholas of Tolentino.* [1]

Christian perfection is nothing other than a renunciation
of the world, the flesh and self-will. This is a truth which
has been stated so many, many times in Holy Scripture and
by the ancient Fathers that it seems there is no need to
repeat it. That great Father of the spiritual life, Cassian,
speaking of this perfection, says that its base and foundation is simply a perfect renunciation of all human will. And
St. Augustine, speaking of those who consecrate themselves
to God in order to tend to this perfection, writes: "What
are these people? Nothing but an assemblage of persons
enrolled in the militia to war and fight against the world,
the flesh and themselves."

Our gentle Lord and Saviour is the Head, Defender and
Captain, not only of this army but also of each combatant.
Now, although the Eternal Father has constituted and
declared Him the Commanding Officer of this army [*Ps.*
2:6], and the one sovereign Captain of it, nevertheless there

is so much gentleness and mercy in the Heart of our dear Master that He desired that others should share in the glory of being leaders in this militia. Especially was the sacred Virgin chosen to be the principal captainess[2] of the female sex, although Our Lord does not cease to be their absolute Master and Commanding Officer, and this in a sovereign degree. When God created Adam He made him father of all humankind, of men and of women equally. Nevertheless He created the woman, whom we call our mother Eve, as the captainess of the female sex. This does not mean that Adam failed to be the absolute head of both sexes. Oh no! But Eve shared in some manner the glory that Adam received.

Indeed, when God delivered the Israelites from Egypt to lead them into the Promised Land He placed them under the hand and guidance of Moses, who was named the captain and leader of this people. And when, by divine inspiration, he commanded his whole army to pass through the Red Sea to escape the fury and tyranny of Pharaoh who pursued it, the sea, separating, left the way dry and free for the Israelites and swallowed up and submerged the Egyptians. [*Ex.* 14:26-31]. Seeing this, Moses entoned his beautiful canticle with an inconceivable interior feeling, accompanied by fifes, oboes, drums and flageolets.

But Sacred Scripture remarks that at the very same time Miriam, his sister, sang the same canticle with those of her sex, as their captainess and leader. They also had fifes and flageolets. [*Ex.* 15:1-21]. It was not that Moses was not the ruler and head of the whole army, of the women equally as well as of the men, but that Miriam, his sister, shared in this glory since she was the leader of those of her own sex. This was not done only for the sake of decorum and propriety, but, as Scripture remarks, according to the order of God, who often showed by means of figures and examples the favors and graces He would bestow on the sacred Virgin, Our Lady.[3]

Now Divine Providence has permitted that while we are

yet in the octave of the Nativity of this Holy Virgin, these young girls have requested to be received, one to the habit and the other to profession. Oh, how great is their enterprise! For it is a struggle and a continual warfare against the world, the flesh and themselves that they have undertaken under the standard and protection of our dearest Mistress. That is why we must consider how this holy Virgin triumphed valiantly over these three adversaries from her first entrance into this life, her holy nativity. Certainly this glorious Lady has been a mirror and an abridgment of Christian perfection; but though God allowed her to pass through all the states of life and degrees of perfection to serve as an example for all people, still is she the special model of the religious life.

In the beginning of her life she was subject to her mother. She remained with her family to show girls and children the honor and subjection they owe their parents and in what spirit they should live in their own homes. She was presented in the Temple in her youth, when only three years old,[4] to teach fathers and mothers the care they should take in rearing their children and with what affection they ought to instruct them in the fear of God and lead them to His service. In this she was also an example for young girls who consecrate themselves to the Divine Majesty. Then she was married, to be a mirror for the married, and finally a widow. Thus Divine Providence let her pass through all the states of life in order that all creatures might find in her, as in a sea of grace, what they need in order to form and adapt themselves to their state in life.

It is true nevertheless, as I have said, that she was the mirror of the religious life particularly; for from her birth she practiced most excellently that perfect renunciation of the world, the flesh and herself, in which Christian perfection consists. As to the world, at her birth the sacred Virgin made the most perfect and entire renunciation that could be made.

What is the world but an inordinate affection for

material things, for life, for honors, dignities, high positions, self-esteem and such like baubles after which worldlings run and of which they become idolaters. I do not
know how this has happened, but the world has entered so
deeply into the heart of man that man has become the
world and the world man. The ancient philosophers seemed
to mean this when they called man a microcosm or little
world. And St. Augustine, speaking of the world, said:
"What is the world? It is nothing other than man; and man,
he is nothing else but the world—as if he meant: Man has
so placed and attached his affections to honors, wealth,
dignities, high positions and self-esteem, that he has, for
that reason, lost the name of man and has received that of
the world. And the world has so powerfully attracted the
affections and appetites of man to itself that it is no longer
called the world, but man.

It is of this world or of these men that the great Apostle
speaks when he writes: The world "did not know" God,
and for that reason it "did not accept Him" [*Jn.* 1:10-11,
17:25; *1 Cor.* 1:21, 2:6-8] nor wish to hear His laws—still
less to receive and keep them, since they are entirely contrary to its own. On this subject Our Lord Himself said: "I
do not pray," My Father, "for the world" with an
efficacious prayer, for the world does not know Me and I
do not know the world. [*Jn.* 17:9]. O God! How difficult it
is to be well detached from this world! Our affections are
so entangled in it and our heart is so sullied from it that
great care is needed to wash and cleanse it well if we do
not want it to remain always sullied and disfigured. Some
think they have already done much and have worked hard
at the exercise of renunciation of and separation from the
world—but alas! They discover that they were really
deluded in this; for however little we examine ourselves, we
find that we are very much apprentices, and we see that
what we have done is nothing in comparison to what we
should have done and what we ought to do.

This is why all the heads and founders of religious orders, in whom reigned the spirit of God, which governed and guided them in their enterprises, all began with this principle. The great St. Francis [of Assisi], entering a church, heard these words of the Gospel: Go, sell your possessions and give to the poor, and follow Me. [*Matt.* 19:21]. He obeyed and began his Rule with this renunciation. St. Anthony, hearing the same words, left all things and did what these words required of him.

And that glorious St. Nicholas of Tolentino, whose feast we celebrate today, was converted when he heard a religious of St. Augustine preaching in church on these words of St. John the Evangelist: The world is passing away.[5] [*1 Jn.* 2:17]. The preacher ardently exhorted the people not to fix their affections on its pomps and vanities, saying: I beg you, my very dear brothers, do not be attached to the world either in your heart or affections, for the heavens and the earth will pass away [*Matt.* 24:35; *Rev.* 21:1,4], with all that is found therein; what it presents to you makes but a brief appearance, but certainly they are only flowers which fade away and are already withered. [*Sir.* 14:18; *Is.* 40:6; *James* 1:10-11]. If you choose to remain in the world, use the things found there, enjoy them and take what you require; but, for the love of God, do not fix your affections on them nor attach yourself to them so that you forget the heavenly and eternal goods for which you were created, for all these things will pass away. [Cf. *1 Cor.* 7:31]. The great St. Nicholas, hearing these words, left all, became a religious of St. Augustine, and lived and died holy.

It is true that it is a good deal to give up the world and withdraw from its bustle to enter religious life as these girls are doing; but certainly we must withdraw from it not only our bodies, but also our hearts. Some who enter monasteries retain an affection for honors, dignities, high places, distinctions and the pleasures of the world, and what they cannot possess in effect they possess in their hearts and desires. This is a great misfortune. On this point I must tell you something I remember having read.[6]

The good man Syncleticus was a great senator who gave up his position to become a monk; but what he no longer possessed in effect he possessed in his heart, and his thoughts wandered among delights, pleasures, honors and suchlike worldly tinsel. Knowing this, the great St. Basil wrote him a letter in which he addressed him in these terms: "Father Syncleticus, what have you done? (*'Quid fecisti?'*) What are you doing, or what have you done? You left the world and your position as a senator to become a monk; but what have you done? At this moment you are neither senator nor monk. You are not a senator, since you left that position to become a monk; therefore it is no longer yours. You are not a monk, because your affections are running after the things of the world. Now you must not act like this, for to be a monk it is not enough to wear a monk's habit; you must unite your affections intimately to God[7] and live in perfect self-denial of the world and all that belongs to it." Do you see where Christian perfection begins? With this renunciation and self-denial.

O God, it is admirable how absolutely and perfectly the sacred Virgin, Our Lady and Mistress, made this renunciation at her nativity! Come close to her cradle, think of the virtues of this holy infant and you will find that she practiced them all to an eminent degree. Question the angels, the cherubim and seraphim, ask them if they are equal in perfection to this little girl, and they will tell you that she infinitely surpasses them. See them surround her cradle, and hear how, lost in wonder at the beauty of this Lady, they say these words of the Song of Songs: Who is this coming up from the desert, like a column of smoke laden with myrrh, with frankincense, and with the fragrant perfume of every exotic dust? [*Song* 3:6].

Then as they regard her a little more closely, ravished and beside themselves, they proceed in their admiration: Who is this that comes forth like the dawn, as beautiful as the moon, as resplendent as the sun, as awe-inspiring as bannered troops? [*Song* 6:10]. This girl is not yet glorified, but glory is promised to her; she awaits it, not in hope as others do, but with assurance. And thus they continue their praises.

There she was, that sacred and blessed Virgin, practicing all the virtues, but in an admirable manner that of renunciation of the world. For amid these praises and this exaltation see how she abases herself, not wishing to appear other than as a simple and ordinary infant, even though she had the use of reason from the very moment of her Conception.

I find three children who had the use of reason before their birth, but differently. The first is St. John the Baptist who was sanctified in his mother's womb, where he recognized Our Lord, "leapt for joy" at His coming, and adored Him. [*Lk.* 1:41,44]. Now this use of reason was not taken away from him, for God bestows His gifts absolutely, without any revocation or recall. [*Rom.* 11:29]. When He gives His grace to a soul He gives it forever and never takes it away unless he to whom He granted it himself desires to lose it. It is the same with His other gifts, which are not taken away from us except through our own demerits.

The second child was our Saviour and Sovereign Master, who had the use of reason from the moment of His Incarnation. O God, may it never happen that the slightest doubt contrary to this be entertained by our understanding for so much as a moment! Now, His life was a life all holy and glorious, for His most blessed soul continually enjoyed the clear vision of the Divinity with which it was united from the moment of its creation.

The third child was the sacred Virgin, who is in the middle between those two. For she did not have the use of reason in the same manner as our Saviour; that belonged to Him alone. But she did have it in a more excellent manner than St. John the Baptist, since she was chosen for a dignity greater than that of this saint. It is true that St. John was to be the Precursor of the Son of God, but the sacred

Virgin was chosen to be the Mother of God.

The great Apostle St. Paul, who is certainly admirable in all that he said, offered an argument by which we can understand how great is the dignity of the Mother of God: Is there an angel, even a seraphim, to whom the Eternal Father has said: "This one is My Son"?[8] [*Heb.* 1:5]. Oh no! That applied only to our dear Saviour and Master who was His true and natural Son. And we can add: Is there any creature to whom the Son of God has said, "My Mother"? No, certainly, that was due to this Virgin alone, who had carried Him for nine months in her sacred womb. Let us conclude then, following this great saint, that the greatest title that can be given to the Holy Virgin is to name her Mother of God.

Now there can be no doubt that, being chosen for a higher dignity than that of St. John, she had the use of reason in a more excellent manner. We other poor people are born in the greatest misery imaginable, for in our infancy we are like animals that can neither talk nor reason. It is because of this that when philosophers are asked: "What is man?" they answer, "He is an animal who can reason." Aristotle said that bees are born as little larvae and then develop wings and finally become bees; but their king is not born in this manner: he is born as king. We are certainly similar, for we are born like little larvae, weak and powerless; but the sacred Virgin was born as our Queen, with the use of reason, and in this birth she already made the same renunciation she would later make with so much perfection.

And who will not marvel to see this heavenly infant in this cradle, capable of knowledge and of love, communicating with and cleaving to God, and in this adherence willing and accepting to be treated by everyone as a simple infant and in every way like unto others. O God! What a sacrifice of glory, pomp and worldly display is this! And concealed so perfectly that this marvel was in no way perceived! Infants are charming in their infancy and innocence, for they love nothing, are attached to nothing, know nothing about points of honor or reputation, or blame and contempt. They make as much of glass as of crystal, of copper as of gold, of imitation rubies as of precious ones. They will give up something very valuable for an apple. That is all lovable in infants; however it is not admirable, since they do not have the use of reason. But in the Holy Virgin, who, appearing as a little infant and acting in all ways as they do, had nevertheless the same power of communicating and of reasoning as when she died—O God, this is not only lovable and pleasing, but most admirable! This, then, was the first renunciation she made.

The second renunciation was that of the flesh. There is no doubt that this is still more difficult than the other, since it is of a higher degree. Many leave the world and even withdraw their affection from it, but have great difficulty in subduing the flesh. For this reason the great Apostle said: Beware of that mortal enemy that always accompanies you, and be on guard lest it seduce you. [*Rom.* 7:23; *Gal.* 5:16-17]. What is this enemy of whom St. Paul speaks? It is the flesh which we carry about with us always, and whether we drink, eat or sleep, this flesh always accompanies us and tries to deceive us. For you see it is the most disloyal, most treacherous and perfidious enemy that can be named, and so the continual renunciation we must make of it is certainly most difficult. Great courage is necessary to undertake this struggle; but to encourage ourselves for it let us cast our eyes on our Head and Sovereign Captain, and on our captainess, the sacred Virgin.

As to Our Lord, He accomplished this abnegation of the flesh in a most excellent manner; His entire holy life was nothing but a continual mortification and renunciation of it. And although His sacred flesh was quite subject to the spirit and never rebelled, nevertheless He did not fail to mortify it, to give us an example and to teach us how we ought to treat our flesh which "lusts against the spirit." [*Rom.* 7:23; *Gal.* 5:16-17]. The lesson which our dear

Master gives us in this is that we should not transform the spirit into flesh and afterwards lead a bestial and subhuman life, but that we should transform our flesh into spirit to lead a life entirely spiritual and divine. This is achieved by means of mortification and continual renunciation. O God! If Our Lord treated His most holy flesh so harshly, He who had not a single bad inclination, shall we who have been so disloyal, treacherous and wicked, refuse and be slow to mortify it in order to subject it to the spirit? [Cf. *1 Pet.* 3:18]. Considering what our Head and Captain has done, are we going to be cowardly soldiers, weak in courage?

The sacred Virgin made this renunciation of the flesh most perfectly in her cradle. It is true that little infants make a thousand acts of renunciation, for they are compelled to it in hundreds of ways; because of the very great care we take of them they are never free to follow their feelings and inclinations. See this poor little baby, he will hold an apple, and for fear lest he eat it and then become sick it is taken from him, and often forcefully. He wishes to stretch out his little arms—they are folded back. He wishes to play with his little feet—and we cover them up. He wishes to see the sunlight—but he is covered up for fear that he will look at it. He wants to stay awake and he is rocked to sleep. In short, he is contradicted in everything. Nevertheless, infants are certainly not to be praised for all this, for they have not the use of reason. But the sacred Virgin, who did have the use of reason in a very perfect manner, voluntarily endured all these mortifications and contradictions in her infancy. And this is how she made the second renunciation.

The glorious Father, St. Augustine, has always been happy in his children, both men and women religious. For they have all tried to follow and imitate him as closely as possible. At present we will speak only of St. Nicholas of Tolentino, his true and legitimate [spiritual] son. From the time this great saint became a religious until the end of his life, he renounced the flesh in a wholly admirable manner, treating his body so rigorously and with so much severity that in this particular point he should be admired rather than imitated.

That is what is practiced in religion. Thus, we come to religious life that we might crucify our flesh and our senses, and that is what these young girls are taught when they enter. We tell them they must crucify their eyes to see nothing, their ears to hear nothing, their tongues to say nothing. You will see a veil placed on their heads not only to teach them that they are dead to the world and its vanities, but also to remind them that henceforth they are to keep their eyes lowered and to look on the earth from which they are molded, to make it clear to them that they have come here to walk in a spirit of humility.

Now although these young girls aspire to Heaven as the place where the only Object of their heart is, nevertheless they are not told to raise their eyes to regard it but rather to look upon the earth where they do not wish to linger. In this they imitate pilots and oarsmen who, to guide their vessel well, do not look to the place where they wish to land but rather turn their back on it. Guiding their barque in this manner, they finally arrive safely. These souls do the same: Looking at the earth in order to humble and confound themselves they attain to Heaven, which is a most secure port. Their ears cannot be seen, so as to teach them that they ought to have them only to hear these words of the Sacred Spouse: Hear, O daughter, and see; turn your ear.

And what does He say? Forget your people and your father's house. [*Ps.* 45:11]. What is signified by the silence they keep except that they have a tongue only to sing with Moses that beautiful canticle of the divine mercy[9] [*Ex.* 15:1-21], which has not only withdrawn them like the Israelites from the tyranny of Pharaoh, that is to say from the devil who held them in slavery and servitude, but has also saved them from being swallowed up in the waves of the Red Sea of their iniquities.

As to the third renunciation, which is the most important of all, namely self-renunciation, it is much more difficult than the other two. We can sometimes reach the perfection of the other two but where there is question of leaving oneself, that is to say, our own spirit, our own soul, our own judgment—even in good things which seem to us better than what has been ordered us—in order to subject ourselves in everything to the guidance of another, here is where there is question of giving up something that is good. Nevertheless this is the aim in religion, for in this consists Christian perfection: to die to self so perfectly that we can say with the Apostle: The life I live now is not my own; Christ is living in me. [*Gal.* 2:20].

Now the practice of this renunciation ought to be continual, for as long as you live you will always find something of yourself to renounce. And this renunciation will be so much the more excellent as you make it with greater fervor. We must not grow weary in this work, for we ought to begin and end the spiritual life with the renunciation of our self-will. Do not deceive yourselves, then, on this point, for if you come into religion with your own spirit you will often be in trouble and interior agitation, since you will find here a spirit completely opposed to your own. It will resist your spirit at every turn until you are completely rid of self-will. Therefore you must be courageous and enter here with this determination. And, although you may suffer something, you will not take alarm, because it cannot be otherwise.

St. Paul speaks marvelously well of this renunciation when he says: The life I live now is not my own; Christ is living in me. As if he had said: Although I am a man of flesh I do not live according to the flesh, but according to the spirit [Cf. *Rom.* 8:12-13]; and not according to my own spirit but according to that of Jesus Christ who lives and reigns in me. Now this great Apostle did not reach this perfect renunciation of self without having suffered many pains and much agitation. Scripture bears witness to this.

[*2 Cor.* 12:7,9-10]. Notice that this self-renunciation consists in giving up our own will, our own spirit, and submitting it to that of another. The angels became devils and stumbled into Hell because they did not wish to submit to God. For, although they did not have a human soul, nevertheless they did have their own spirit, and being unwilling to renounce it and make it subject and submissive to their Creator, they were miserably lost. It is true that all our happiness consists in this subjection of our own spirit, as on the contrary all our unhappiness comes from a lack of it.

Devout persons in the world to a certain extent make the first two renunciations of which we have spoken. But as to this one, certainly it is done only in religion. For although the laity renounce the world and the flesh and subject themselves to a certain degree, they always keep something back. They all reserve for themselves at least the liberty of choosing spiritual exercises. But in religion we renounce everything and submit ourselves in everything, since in giving up our liberty we renounce absolutely the choice of our exercises of devotion, to follow the course of the community.

The most holy Virgin made this last renunciation in her nativity in such a way that she never used her liberty. Consider well the whole course of her life and you will see nothing but continual subjection. She went to the Temple, but it was her parents who brought her there, for they had promised her to God. Shortly after, they gave her in marriage. See her leaving Nazareth to go to Bethlehem, her flight into Egypt, her return to Nazareth. In short, you will see in all her comings and goings only an admirable subjection and docility. She went so far as to see her Son and her God die on the wood of the Cross, remaining firm and standing at the foot of it, submitting herself to the Divine decree by adhering to the will of the Eternal Father. Not by compulsion, but of her own free will, she approved and consented to the death of Our Lord. She kissed a hundred thousand times the Cross to which He was attached, she embraced it and adored it. O God! What abnegation is this! It is true that the tenderly loving heart of this Sorrowful Virgin was transpierced by vehement sorrows. [*Lk.* 2:35]. Who could describe the pains and disturbances which then passed through that sacred heart! Nevertheless we see that it was sufficient for this holy Lady to know that it was the will of the Eternal Father that His Son should die and also that she should see Him die, to keep her standing firm at the foot of the Cross [*Jn.* 19:25], as approving and accepting His death.

St. Augustine, speaking of the rod of Jesse at the end of a long and beautiful discourse which I will not repeat because of its length (it would take an infinite amount of time), said that this rod resembled the almond, which he compared to Our Lord. I will end this exhortation here by demonstrating how excellently our dear Master and Saviour practiced this abnegation. St. Augustine explained that there are three remarkable things about the almond. The first is the covering, which is very rough. The second is the shell or the wood which surrounds the nut. The third is the nut.

The outer covering represents the humanity of Our Lord, which was so blackened and bruised from the blows He received that He said He was "a worm, not a man." [*Ps.* 22:7]. The nut, which is not only sweet and good to eat, but when crushed is even better for making oil to brighten and illuminate, represents the Divinity. The shell symbolizes the wood of the Cross to which Our Lord was attached and by which He was so crushed that He gave forth the oil of mercy. This has also enlightened the world in such a way that it has delivered it from its darkness and ignorance.

It was on this wood that our dear Saviour and Sovereign Captain made this perfect renunciation of Himself. It is to this Cross that all the saints were attached. The sorrows of the Cross were the special subjects of their prayers. Certainly the true religious ought always to have the Cross and the crucifix before his eyes to learn from it how to give up and renounce himself. Although the goodness of Our Lord is so great that He sometimes lets us taste the sweetness of His Divinity, granting some grace and favor to our souls, nevertheless for that very reason we ought never to forget the bitterness that He suffered for us in His humanity. I have said and I will say and I will not grow weary of repeating that religion is "a Mount Calvary" where we must crucify ourselves with Our Lord and Master in order to reign with Him.

Let us conclude with the glorious St. Nicholas of Tolentino who made these three renunciations of which we have spoken. Having indeed crucified himself on the Cross of our Saviour, he desired at the hour of his death that this sacred wood be brought to him. Seeing it and embracing it he cried out as another St. Andrew: "O good Cross, O Cross so long desired; Hail, O Cross! O unique Cross, O precious Cross—resting and leaning on this as upon a secure staff, I shall pass with dry feet through the stormy sea of this world." Being completely transformed by the sorrows of Our Lord, he merited to have this Divine Saviour appear to him at the hour of his death, with one arm resting on the sacred Virgin and the other on St. Augustine. Jesus Christ then said to him: Come, My faithful servant; you who have served Me so well under the Rule which I gave your founder. Come! Possess the crown which has been prepared for you. [Cf. *Lk.* 19:17; *James* 1:12].

Oh, how happy you will be, my dear daughters, if you make this absolute renunciation of the world, of the flesh and of yourself. How happy you will be if from now on you live in the exact observance of the Rules and Constitutions which have been given you on the part of God. In doing this, without doubt you will have the same favor that St. Nicholas received from Our Lord, Our Lady and St. Augustine, since you are daughters of the same Father and the same Mother as he.[10] If you have faithfully kept your Rules, the Saviour will assuredly come with the sacred Virgin to receive you at the hour of your death, if not visibly—for that must not be desired—at least invisibly, to introduce you into eternal life. May the Father, the Son and the Holy Spirit lead you there! Amen.

NOTES

1. St. Francis de Sales preached this sermon during a ceremony in which one Visitation nun took the religious habit, becoming a novice, and another was professed. In the liturgical calendar of that time, the feast of Mary's Nativity (September 8) was celebrated with an octave, and September 10th was the feast of St. Nicholas of Tolentino. St. Francis weaves all these themes together in this sermon.
2. "Captainess": St. Francis de Sales used the French suffix "esse" to create the feminine word "captainess" in order to demonstrate the intimate cooperation of the Virgin Mary with her Son in the plan of salvation.
3. In the French of the Annecy edition of this sermon, "Miriam" is rendered "Marie," making the allusion to Our Lady even more pronounced.
4. Cf. Sermon for Nov. 21, 1617, p. 37.
5. Cf. *Conferences,* XVII, "On Voting," p. 324, note 2.
6. Cf. Sermon for Nov. 21, 1617, p. 45.
7. Cf. *Conferences,* XX, p. 388.
8. Cf. Sermon for Aug. 15, 1618, p. 67.
9. Cf. above, p. 101.
10. The Rule of St. Augustine forms the basis for the Rules of many religious congregations and orders. In 1618, when the Congregation of the Visitation was erected into a religious order, it was placed by its founder under the Rule of St. Augustine. "Father" here no doubt refers to him, as "Mother" refers to Mary.

THE PRESENTATION OF OUR LADY
IN THE TEMPLE

Sermon for the Feast of the Presentation of Our Lady, November 21, 1620, concerning the significance of the Old Testament laver (water basin) between the two tabernacles: Baptism, penance, evangelical doctrine; the body and the soul, Mary's infancy and childhood, the blessedness of Mary's Divine Motherhood and of having heard the word of God and kept it, religious vocation, partial and total giving of self to God, the two conditions of true obedience, and continual renewal of vows.

"See that you make them according to the pattern shown you on the mountain."—Ex. 25:40

In the Old Law the Divine Majesty commanded Moses to build the Ark and to erect the tabernacle according to the details which He described very minutely when He spoke to him "on the mountain." [*Ex.* 25ff]. This was done, but in a manner so admirable that there was nothing, even in the smallest design, that was not full of great mysteries. The ancient Fathers, after considering it all, pause with admiration at the most abject and meanest part of all; for among other things God had ordained that a laver be put between the exterior tabernacle in which the people who came to offer sacrifices remained, and the interior tabernacle where the priests of the Law stayed; or rather between the two altars, that is, between the altar of holocausts and the altar of incense. The Divine Majesty then commanded Moses to make a "bronze laver" which should be filled with water in order that the priests of the Law might wash their hands and feet before they went to offer sacrifices; and for its embellishment they should surround it entirely with mirrors like those of the Jewish ladies. [*Ex.* 30:18-20; 38:8].

Now, our ancient Fathers have given so great a number of interpretations on this laver and on these mirrors that if I were to speak a word on each one it would take me an entire hour. I shall discuss only three of their conceptions: first, what this laver signifies and what we must understand by it; second, why it was between the two tabernacles; and third, what the mirrors which surround it represent.

As to the first point, a large number of the ancient Fathers say this laver represents Baptism and for that reason it was placed between the exterior and interior tabernacle. Certainly they have reasons for this opinion, for no one can enter the interior tabernacle, which is none other than Heaven, without passing through the exterior one, which is the Church, to which belongs this laver full of the baptismal waters in which we must be plunged and cleansed. These waters purify, justify and remove all the stains of sin with which people are defiled; and in order to offer and sacrifice any victim and holocaust to Our Lord it is so necessary to be washed clean by this water, actually or at least by a very ardent desire for it, that without this all offerings and oblations are not offerings but execrations.

Some other Fathers hold that this laver represents penance, and it seems to me that these come even closer to the truth; for what else is penance if not the water in which it is very expedient that we should wash our feet and our hands, that is to say our affections and works, soiled and stained by so many sins and imperfections? O my dear friends, it is true that the only door by which we may enter Heaven is the Redemption, without which we should never have had access there. But in order that this Redemption may be applied to us we must do penance. We must not deceive ourselves, for our forefathers have all passed by that way: young and old, small and great; in short, all have washed their feet and their hands in the waters of penance.

This is so universal a rule that no one can be exempted from it except the most sacred Virgin who, not having sinned, had no need of expiation; and nevertheless she has not entered Heaven by any other door than that of the Redemption. But as for the rest of us it is necessary, as I have said, to do penance either in this world or in the next. I know indeed that there is one penance to which mortal sins oblige us and another we must do for venial sins. All the same, penance is absolutely necessary for both of them, and the one who does not do it in this life will undoubtedly do it in the next. That is why, say the Fathers, this laver was between the two tabernacles, the exterior and the interior, in order to signify that the waters of penance are between the exterior tabernacle of the Church Militant and the interior tabernacle of the Church Triumphant, and that to pass from the Militant to the Triumphant we must be cleansed in these waters.

Others have said that this laver represents evangelical doctrine. Certainly they are right, for this doctrine is nothing else than the water of which anyone who drinks will never be thirsty again, and, as Our Lord said: It will leap up to provide eternal life. [*Jn.* 4:14]. It is in this sacred water that we must immerse all our members, that is to say, cleanse our works and affections in order to purify them, and form and adjust them according to the Law of the Gospel. Without this we can make neither oblation nor sacrifice, and still less can we be saved except by believing [*Mk.* 16:16] this Christian doctrine and forming ourselves according to it. It is there that we see what we must believe, ask for, and hope for.

Let no one be deceived on this point by thinking to reach this interior tabernacle, there to offer sacrifices of thanksgiving [*Ps.* 116:17], without washing himself in these waters or molding himself on this doctrine. For no one can be saved by making laws according to one's own caprice or fancy or by contenting oneself with the natural law. No indeed, that cannot be. You see, then, that this laver placed between the tabernacles represents Baptism, penance, and evangelical doctrine, which are the bonds by which the Church Militant is united to the Church Triumphant.

We ourselves also have two tabernacles: the one exterior, which is this body that we carry with us, and the other interior, which is the soul by which we live. This is what the great Apostle St. Paul [*2 Cor.* 5:1, 4] wished to say: Our bodies are tabernacles or tents made and formed of potter's clay, and God has enclosed in them great treasures. [*2 Cor.* 4:7]. What are these treasures if not our souls which, as interior tabernacles, are hidden in our bodies? But as the soul animates and gives life to the body, so does evangelical doctrine nourish and vivify the soul, furnishing it with light and strength to guide it and bring it to that other more interior tabernacle where the Most High dwells.

Certainly a day will come when we shall rise from the dead, and these mortal bodies which we have, now subject to corruption, will be immortal, entirely spiritual [*1 Cor.* 15:51-54] and remade like that of Our Lord. [*Phil.* 3:21]. Then with unspeakable joy we shall see them made all glorious by their reunion with the soul, against which there will be no more rebellion or variance; rather, they will be absolutely submissive and subject to it. The soul will so possess them that it will govern them sovereignly. And as to our bodies, they will participate in the glory of the soul; by this means that which is mortal will be made immortal like the soul.

This laver was completely surrounded by mirrors. These mirrors represent the examples of the saints who, having received the Christian doctrine, practiced it so perfectly and completely that we may say that the stories of their lives are as so many mirrors which decorate and enrich this laver of the evangelical Law. And just as this Law has decorated and enriched them, and they, by plunging themselves into it, have been purified and rendered capable of offering to the Divine Goodness sacrifices of an inestimable price and value, so have they on their side done for it what the mirrors of the Hebrew and Jewish women did for that ancient laver. For they have embellished it by the practice of the precepts and counsels which they have drawn from it, permitting us to imitate their admirable examples which are like mirrors in which we may continually look into ourselves. For, although we do not need mirrors like the Hebrew women to admire our bodies, which will decay with the dogs and other animals, nevertheless we must always have before our eyes the mirrors of the virtues and examples of the saints in order to pattern and form all our actions on them. Now I am at the subject of the feast of our most dear Mother and Mistress which we celebrate today. For, I ask you, what more beautiful and precious mirror could be presented to you than this one? Is it not the most excellent one there is in the evangelical doctrine? Has she not ornamented and enriched it the most, as much by what she herself has practiced as by the admirable examples that she has left us? Certainly there is not a saint that can be ranked with her, for this glorious Virgin surpasses in dignity and excellence not only the saints but also the highest seraphim and cherubim. She has a great advantage over all the blessed in that she has entirely given and dedicated herself to the service of God from the instant of her Conception, since there is no doubt that she was all pure and had the use of reason as soon as her soul was infused into that little body formed in the womb of St. Anne.

As this glorious Virgin was born of a father and mother like other children, so it seems that like them she must be defiled with Original Sin. But for her, Divine Providence ordained quite the contrary, and extending His most holy hand, held her back for fear that she might fall into this precipice. He gave her the use of reason and faith by which Our Lady knew God and believed all revealed truth in such a way that, filled with this light, she dedicated and consecrated herself completely to the Divine Majesty, and in a most perfect manner. Theologians assure us that Our Lord, casting a ray of His light and grace into the soul of St. John the Baptist when he was still in the womb of St. Elizabeth, sanctified him and gave him the use of reason with the gift of faith by which, having recognized his God in the womb of the most holy Virgin, he adored Him and consecrated himself to His service. If the Saviour gave such a grace to the one who was to be His Precursor, who can doubt that He not only bestowed the same favor but that He also granted a much greater and more particular privilege to her whom He had chosen to be His Mother? Why would He not have sanctified her from her mother's womb [*Ps.* 71:6, 139:13], as indeed He did St. John?[1]

It is then an assured fact that from the instant of her Conception God rendered her all-pure, all-holy, with the perfect use of faith and reason in a wonderful manner that cannot be sufficiently admired. For He had this intention from all eternity because His thoughts are as high as the heavens are above the earth [*Is.* 55:8-9], and that which could never enter human understanding God has meditated upon before the beginning of time. Oh, how many were the favors, graces and blessings that the Divine Goodness poured into the heart of the glorious Virgin! But they were so secret and interior that no one could have known of them but she who experienced them—and her mother, St. Anne; for we may believe that, at the instant that the Lord poured so many graces into the soul of this blessed child, the mother felt them in herself and experienced great sweetness and spiritual consolations on account of her daughter on whom they were lavished.

I shall not speak at this time either of what our most dear Mistress and Mother did at her Conception and nativity, or of the blessings she then received. I wish to treat only of this feast on which she came to offer and con-

secrate herself to the service of the Temple. O God, how
blessed she was, for she was only three years old when she
left her country and her father's house.[2] [*Gen.* 12:1; *Ps.*
45:11]. She was like a beautiful flower that sheds its perfume early in the morning. There are two kinds of flowers
that give forth their perfume differently: roses and pinks.
Roses are more fragrant in the morning and their perfume
is sweeter at that time; on the contrary, pinks have more
perfume in the evening and their scent is stronger and more
pleasing. Certainly this glorious Virgin has been like a
beautiful rose among thorns; and although she always gave
forth an odor of perfect sweetness during her entire life, yet
in the morning of her sweet childhood she shed a scent that
was marvelously sweet.

This loving darling was no sooner born than she began
to use her little tongue to sing the praises of the Lord and
all her other little members to serve Him. His Divine
Goodness inspired her to leave her father and mother's
house and go to the Temple, there to serve Him more perfectly. In her parents' house this glorious Virgin comported
herself at this early age with so much wisdom and discretion that she astounded her parents so that they concluded,
as much by her speech as by her actions, that this child
was not like others, but that she had the use of reason, and
therefore they should anticipate the time and lead her to
the Temple to serve the Lord with the other girls who were
there for that purpose. So they took this little Virgin at the
age of only three years, leading her, and for part of the
way carrying her, to the Temple of Jerusalem.

O God, how great were the sighs and aspirations of love
and dilection that this little maid uttered—her father and
mother too—but she above all, for it was she who was
going to sacrifice herself anew to her Divine Spouse who
had inspired her and called her to this retreat, not only in
order to receive her as His spouse but also to prepare her
to be His Mother! Oh, how sweetly she went, singing that
sacred song of the Psalmist: *Beati immaculati in via.* [*Ps.*

119]. ("Happy are they whose way is blameless, who walk in the law of the Lord."). This psalm is certainly admirable and as sweet as honey on account of the words of praise and benediction that it renders to the Divine Majesty. As the Royal Prophet said: I use this canticle as a sweet recreation, intoning and singing it the three different times that I go to the Temple, according to the ordinance of the Law. [*Ps.* 118:54, *Douay*]. The Hebrew and Jewish women also sang it with great devotion when they went there. But who could explain with what emotions of love and dilection this holy Virgin recited it, especially as this sacred canticle does not treat of anything but the Law and Will of God,[3] to obey which she made her way to the Temple?

Many Hebrew and Jewish women had dedicated themselves to the divine service in this way, but not one of them had approached the perfection of this glorious Virgin. She offered and consecrated herself with so much fervor, love and humility that the angels and the highest seraphim who promenaded on the balustrade and gallery of Heaven were enraptured, astonished that a creature so pure could be found on earth, and that a soul clothed with a human body could make so perfect an offering and oblation. It is true that we may say of her what the Holy Spirit recounts [*1 Kgs.* 10:1-2,10] of the Queen of Sheba when she went to see Solomon: She came laden with so much nard and perfumes that never was so much of it seen in Jerusalem as that which this queen brought. In the same manner, our glorious Virgin came with "such perfumes" of sanctity that never was as much seen in all the women who had dedicated themselves in the Temple as was found in her alone. There she is, then, at this early age, vowed and sacrificed entirely to God.

Oh, how happy are the souls who in imitation of this sacred Virgin dedicate themselves like beginners to the service of Our Lord from their youth! Oh, how happy they are for having retired from the world before the world has known them, because, not having been married, and consequently not blighted by the ardor of concupiscence, they give forth an odor of great sweetness by their virtues and good works. But yet while all souls may aspire to and desire this happiness, nevertheless all do not receive the grace. That is why I am accustomed to say that there are two kinds of childhood. The first is that of which we are now speaking. The other is that by which we correspond promptly to the secret inspirations of God when, rendering ourselves docile to the first movement and attraction of grace at whatever time and age Our Lord calls us, we leave all to follow Him.[4]

This is indeed a great feast that we celebrate today on which this little maid went to offer herself in the Temple in her tender youth and at the first invitation of inspiration. This feast is not at all new, for the Greeks make mention of it. We even read that it has always been celebrated by Oriental Catholics, although in the Orient its celebration had little solemnity. But since Pope Sixtus V re-established it, the Church has solemnized it and given it an office. It is for you, my dear Sisters, a very solemn day, inasmuch as on it you come to offer yourselves to the Divine Majesty in imitation of this glorious Virgin, or rather to renew the offering that you have already made.[5]

But you will say to me: "Speak to us a little on how and with what perfection our divine Mistress made her offering, so that we may imitate her; for being her daughters we shall indeed be glad to follow her." You notice that on this feast we do not have any other Gospel than the one that is read every time the office of Our Lady is said. [*Lk.* 11:27-28]. Now you will find in it all you must do to imitate her.

It is said that Our Lord, preaching to the people who followed Him and wishing to illuminate and enlighten them, performed for this purpose many miracles. The pharisees, full of envy, began to murmur and calumniate Him, saying that it was not in His Name that He did these things but by the power of the prince of darkness. [*Lk.* 11:15]. At the height of these blasphemies and insults "a woman called out" (who the holy Fathers say was St. Marcella,[6] but as the Gospel does not name her, it is better only to say that it was a woman) and, full of admiration for the Divine Master, exclaimed: Blest is the womb that bore You and the breasts that nursed You! Then the people, full of astonishment, were silent; and the Saviour, turning toward this woman, replied: Rather, blest are they who hear the word of God and keep it!

Now, although I remember that I have already spoken to you three or four times on this subject and on this Gospel,[7] nevertheless it is a well from which there is so much to be taken that I cannot keep from speaking of it and drawing from its depths what is proper for our instruction. Blest, she said, are the breasts that gave You milk and the womb that bore You. And Our Lord answered her: It is true that the womb that bore Me is blest and the breasts that nursed Me are happy; for what greater happiness could come to a woman than to bear in her womb Him who is equal to the Father—Him whom the heavens cannot contain?

Oh, how truly blessed is that womb in which the Son of God has taken human flesh, and what an honor this Virgin has received by giving her most pure blood to form the sacred humanity of the Saviour of our souls! Therefore, O woman, what you say is indeed true, that not only this womb but even the breasts that nursed Me are blest, inasmuch as they have nourished that One who sustains all creatures. That great almoner Abraham was considered very highly favored because, in lodging pilgrims, he one day had the grace of having the King and Lord of pilgrims in his house, of eating with Him, and of washing His feet. [*Gen.* 18:1-8]. How much more blessed should we think this womb of the Virgin, which has lodged Him not for only one day but for nine entire months, and those breasts which have nourished Him not with bread but with milk, with the very substance of this glorious Virgin?

Oh, woman, what you say is the truth! That chaste

womb resembles the Ark in which were "the manna, the rod of Aaron which had blossomed, and the tablets of the covenant" of the Law of Moses. [*Heb.* 9:4]. What is that manna if not the Son of God who has come down from Heaven? [*Jn.* 6:31-33]. Is He not also that rod and those tablets of the Law? Yes, He is the "living stone" [*1 Pet.* 2:4]: On His own body have been written and engraved the ten commandments of the law of grace with the points of the nails, the lance, and the lashes. "Oh, how blest then is this womb," Our Lord seems to say, "since it is more precious than the Ark of the Covenant; and therefore how blest is this woman because she is My Mother. And certainly this happiness belongs only to her inasmuch as no other creature, whoever she might be, can or will ever be honored with the title of Mother of God. It belongs only to the sacred Virgin; for in the same manner as, being God, I have only a Father without a mother, so as man I must have a Mother without a father; and as I have only one Father in Heaven, so I must have only one Mother on earth. That has been ordained from all eternity by My Heavenly Father. Nevertheless, I tell you now that although My Mother is so blest because she has borne Me in her womb and I have been nourished from her breasts, yet is she much more blest because she has heard the word of God and kept it. And all can participate in this beatitude."

But consider how this holy Virgin has heard the divine word and how she has kept it. And to pass over every other word and to speak only of that of her vocation, O God, how faithful she has been in this! See how the Lord whispers in her ear, or rather in the interior of her heart: *Audi, filia* —"Listen, O daughter," and see; turn your ear: Forget your country and leave your father's house. So shall the King desire your beauty. [*Ps.* 45:11-12].

Note these words: "Listen, O daughter." It is as if He said: "In order to hear well, one must listen." But besides that, one must bow down and pay attention, that is to say, abase and humble oneself in order to understand what is the will of God. "Forget your country and leave your father's house. Come to the land I will show you. [*Gen.* 12:1]. Then the King will desire your beauty." It is as if He said: "Do not content yourself with listening to the divine inspiration and abasing yourself the better to hear it, but withdraw your heart and your affection from your country and from your family, come to the place that I will show you, and I will desire your beauty."

Oh holy, divine, and admirable invitation which God extends to the heart of so many creatures, and which has been listened to and understood by a great number! However, I do not know how it has happened that many have heard the sacred word of a vocation and have not left nor gone where God called them. They must make so many reflections, they must consider so much, they must speak with first one and then another to find out if the inspiration is true, if it comes from God—everything must be minutely examined! Certainly it is good to weigh and consider well what the inspiration is, but after this glance at it, "Leave and go into the land which" God shows you.[8] Do not listen to so many discourses, do not give ear to so many reasonings that may be brought before you, do not make so many delays, for you put yourself in great peril. Do not sleep; be prompt.

O God, how diligent was the glorious Virgin, and how well may we apply to her this verse of the Psalmist: He "neither slumbers nor sleeps." [*Ps.* 121:4]. She did not sleep, for at this divine word of her vocation she rose up promptly and departed. She had no need of long reflections because she had the grace of discernment. She went where God led her, and the King of Heaven, desiring her beauty, chose her not only for His spouse but also for His Mother.

Thus, "blest are they who hear the word of God and keep it." All are called [*Matt.* 20:16; 22:14; *1 Tim.* 2:4], and many hear the inspiration, differently however—some more, others less. It is like to what happens in the court of some great prince who might be in his palace, surrounded by many lords. They are indeed all in his court and in the presence of the prince, who looks at some, casts more particular glances upon others, smiles at this one, speaks to that one, gives dignities to some, favors others, as I know such or similar things happen every day at the courts of kings. All esteem these favors and make great account of them. But there are those whom the prince favors even more and to whom he witnesses a more particular affection. They are those whom he has enter his cabinet—to converse with them, to disclose to them his secrets and to communicate to them his ideas.

All Christians are these princes and knights who dwell in the court of this Sovereign King Our Lord, which is nothing else but the Church. Our dear Saviour looks at them all. He favors some, He elevates others. In short, He dispenses His graces to whom He pleases and as He pleases. But besides the favors which He bestows on all the children of His Church, there are particular ones for those whom He withdraws into His cabinet, that is to say, into religion. There He speaks more familiarly to their heart, reveals to them His secrets and lets them know His intentions. Of this number was the sacred Virgin. It is she who has been led into the cabinet of God and to whom have been revealed, more than to any other creature, the highest Mysteries. Thus, "blest are they who hear the word of God and keep it."

This is what Isaiah meant when he said that he believed in the word of the Lord[9] [*Is.* 62:2,4], and that he would engrave His Name on his heart; that is, he would hear the inspiration and will of God and keep it in his heart. I know that there are various interpretations of this, for some hold that by this Name we must understand the holy and sacred Name of Jesus which means Saviour, by which He came to save the world. [*Matt.* 1:21; *Lk.* 1:31; *Acts* 4:10,12]. It is the Name which has remained engraved in His Church and in the heart of every one of its true children.

Others have said that these words of Isaiah must be interpreted as applying to the Church itself. Finally, it may be understood that they concern inspiration and the divine will. For it is the characteristic of the true faithful to bear the sacred Name of Jesus engraved in their heart not with any other pen than the nails, lance and thorns which pierced His holy body. And in addition, every good Christian must listen to and keep the word of God, hear His inspiration, and do His will.

But alas, it is a great misfortune that so few really understand these holy inspirations! Many live in the world and use riches, honors and dignities, which the divine law permits them to use but never to abuse. They adjust their affection for the enjoyment of property and dignities to the commandments of God. It would be useless to speak of the counsels to them since they are satisfied only to avoid what could condemn them. These people are happy, however, for they will share in the Kingdom of God.

Others, indeed, really hear the inspiration of God, but they wish to give themselves over to a good time. They propose to dedicate themselves entirely to God, but they wish to reserve something for themselves. Ah, they say, I shall give myself to God, but not so absolutely that the world may not have some part of me. I shall render to God what is His due [*Matt.* 22:21], but I shall reserve for myself what is due to the world, namely my eyes, my hair, and other such trifles, without doing anything contrary to the divine law. These, too, are happy.

Others, indeed, wish to follow the inspiration and will of God. They wish to be all His, but not completely; for there is indeed a difference between belonging all to God, and belonging totally to God. At least they intend to reserve for themselves the choice of their spiritual exercises. For that is good, they say; that is for God. It is in order to serve Him better, and I see that such an exercise is better for me than another. Alas, they put themselves in danger of being seduced and deceived by wishing to govern themselves according to their fancy and not to be submissive, and by reserving for themselves the choice of their exercises or plan of life, which they form according to their caprice. And do you not see that by making this reservation you are not giving yourself totally *to* God? But it is *for* God; granted. However, the glorious Virgin certainly did not act thus, for she gave herself totally to Him on the day of her Presentation, without any reserve, however small it might be. For she never used her own will nor her own choice, not having retained a single bit of it for anything whatever, and she persevered most perfectly in this throughout her life, always belonging totally to her God.

Oh, when we consider the course of this Lady's most holy life, I assure you that our hearts are entirely filled with delight and sweetness! And when we look at the rare examples that she has left us we are overcome with admiration. If we wish to possess this sweetness and even impart it to the heart of our neighbor, we must meditate well upon the life of our divine Mistress.

She must always be before your eyes, my very dear daughters, that you may form your life on hers and make all your actions and affections correspond to hers. You are her daughters. Thus you must follow and imitate her, and make use of her example as of a mirror in which you look at yourself without ceasing. Even though the fragrance which you will receive by looking at and considering the life of Our Lady will fall into a vessel of clay, it will not lack an admirable sweetness, for balm put in earthen vessels is as sweet as that in a crystal vial.

How many marvelous examples of her obedience to God's will has this divine Mother left us! Consider her marriage to St. Joseph, her flight into Egypt. O glorious Virgin, where are you going with this little darling? I am going to Egypt. What makes you go there? God's will. Will it be for a long time? As long as it shall please Him. And when will you return? When God commands it. But will you not be more joyful in returning than in going? Oh, certainly not. And why not? Because I shall be doing God's will equally in going and remaining as well as in returning. But in coming back you will return to your own country. O God, I have no other country but that of accomplishing the divine will.[10] Oh, what an admirable example of obedience! Since I am on the subject of obedience I shall tell you the two fundamental conditions of this virtue, which I shall discuss briefly. The first is that to obey perfectly we must love God who commands; the second is that we must love the thing commanded. All the failings that we commit against obedience ordinarily proceed from a lack of these two conditions. Some love God who commands, but they do not love the thing commanded. Others like the thing commanded and do not love God who commands.

There is a preacher who preaches the word of God. Everyone hurries there. Why? Because he does marvels. There is another who preaches the same word. No one goes there. Ah, they say, this preacher does not please me; he does not have poise; his discourse is not pleasing. Alas, poor people, why is that? He does not have flowery language and the like. Oh! What blindness! Is it not the word and will of God that he preaches to you? Now if you love this divine word, and God who gives it and who commands that you do His will, why will you not receive it with as good a heart from this one as from the other one? If a prince or a king sent you some letters by one of his pages, would you look to see if the page were dressed in gray, green or yellow before being pleased with these letters? No, certainly; you would take these letters and put them on your head as a sign of rejoicing and reverence, without regard for the livery of the one who brought them. Why then do you not listen to and receive the sacred word equally from some as from others?

Many like the thing commanded and do not love God who commands. A girl (for we speak only of your sex at this time) will be ordered to go to prayer or some other exercise that she likes. Certainly she will go willingly. And why? Because she likes it on account of some sweetness and consolation that she finds there. No one says a word to her; she does not speak; she does nothing; no one bothers her; she receives some sweetness there. And it is self-love that does it! It is true. For take her from it and assign her some other things that she does not like and you will see if she does them and if she goes there without sulking. Who does not see that she does not love God who commands, but only the thing commanded? For if she loved God who commands she would love equally the Giver of contradictions and the Giver of consolations.

Another will love God who commands and not the thing commanded. I know indeed, she will say, that the thing which is ordered for me to do is good since it is God's will, but I have so much repugnance and difficulty that I cannot accept it. Furthermore, when I try to like it, the one who orders me in God's Name has such a bad grace and such a sorry expression that he makes it entirely displeasing and repugnant to me. He has so cold and so dry a countenance that no relish can be found in what he commands.

O God, here is the cause of all our troubles.[11] When our superiors and those who govern are to our taste, fancy, and inclination, and according to our dispositions, we find nothing difficult. But if they are not to our liking, the least things ordered by them are displeasing. Whence does this come if not from the fact that we do not look at God who sends us the command, but rather that before agreeing to do it, we consider if the one who brings it is dressed in green or gray, and what is his expression and countenance? Now this is not necessary at all. What is necessary is to see the obedience as God's will, no matter by whom it is given to us, to love God who commands it, and to take this order and put it on our head—that is to say, in the depth of our will, in order to accept and carry it out with fidelity. If our heart feels a repugnance to the thing commanded, we must caress it and make it submit very sweetly. Doing this, we shall imitate the glorious Virgin and make ourselves totally God's.

By your renewal of vows, my dear daughters, you are going to gain new strength and bind yourselves again to the service and good pleasure of Our Lord. For certainly as long as we live we shall have need of renewing ourselves and of beginning over. All the saints have acted thus, and this renovation was practiced even in the Old Law,[12] inasmuch as our nature is so infirm that it easily grows cold and begins to fail. Even the earth relaxes and, at times, does not produce. It rests in winter; but when spring comes it renews itself and we rejoice to see that, having recovered its vigor, it makes us share amply in its flowers and fruits.[13]

Thus, my dear daughters, you come to make your renovation as Our Lady teaches us in her Presentation. She had no need of renewing herself inasmuch as she had not sinned and thus had not become lax. Nevertheless, for our instruction Divine Providence permitted that she should reconfirm on this day the sacrifice she had made to Him at her Conception. Make your renewal, then, with a great fervor of spirit, a profound humility, and an ardent charity. Send forth sighs and darts of love to our dear Saviour. Accompany this glorious Virgin; place your hearts and your vows between her hands and she will present them to her Son, who will receive them and offer them to His Eternal Father, who with Him and the Holy Spirit will bless you. Amen.

NOTES

1. St. Francis de Sales is following here a usual practice in assigning honors to Mary: What can be said of any saint can certainly be affirmed of Mary, the greatest of saints, and to a degree higher than any other saint.
2. Cf. Sermon for Nov. 21, 1617, p. 35-37.
3. Cf. *Treatise,* Bk. 8, ch. 5.
4. Cf. Sermon for Nov. 21, 1617, p. 41-42.
5. The Visitation nuns, to whom St. Francis is preaching this sermon, renew their vows every November 21, the Feast of the Presentation.

6. Cf. Sermon for Nov. 21, 1619, p. 75-76.
7. Cf. Sermon for Aug. 5, 1617, p. 25-27; Sermon for Aug. 15, 1618, p. 64; Sermon for Nov. 21, 1619, p. 75-76.
8. Cf. *Treatise*, Bk. 8, ch. 11.
9. Cf. *Treatise*, Bk. 8, ch. 7.
10. Cf. *Treatise*, Bk. 9, ch. 14.
11. Cf. *Conferences*, XI, "The Virtue of Obedience."
12. Cf. Sermon for Nov. 21, 1619, p. 81.
13. Cf. Sermon for Nov. 21, 1617, p. 40. St. Francis de Sales is demonstrating sound psychological insight here. Human beings must continually renew their determination to do God's will, for in our relationship with God, as well as with others, we are never on "automatic pilot." Our "yes" to those relationships must be renewed again and again, consciously and freely.

— 10 —

THE ANNUNCIATION

*Sermon for a religious Profession on the Feast of
the Annunciation, March 25, 1621, concerning
Our Lady as the spouse described in the Song of
Songs, God as the only true satisfaction for the
heart of man, perfect dedication to God, the in-
timacy with God enjoyed by religious, Mary as the
perfect religious, the excellence of Our Lady's
virginity, virginity and humility, charity and
humility, Our Lady's drawing of young girls to the
life of virginity, the difference between the
religious life as practiced by men and by women,
and Our Lady as exemplar of religious.*

> *"Let Him kiss me with the kiss of His mouth!
> For Your breasts are better than wine, and
> pour forth perfumes of sweet ointments."*—
> Song 1:1-2, Douay

The divine lover,[1] heaving a deep sigh, begins by saying:
Let Him kiss me, this dear Friend of my soul, let Him kiss
me with the kiss of His mouth! For Your breasts are better
than wine, giving forth odors of delicious fragrance. Your
Name is as oil poured out which, being composed of all the
most precious perfumes, gives forth odors delightful above
all others; and that is why the young maidens love You.
Then continuing, she adds: Draw me and we will run after
Your ointments. [*Song 1:3, Douay*].
The Fathers, considering this word of the Song of Songs

which the spouse addresses to her Spouse: "Let Him kiss me with the kiss of His mouth," say that this kiss which she so ardently desires is nothing else but the accomplishment of the Mystery of Our Lord's Incarnation, a kiss so awaited and desired during the long flow of years by all souls who merit the name of lovers. But at length this kiss, which had been so long refused and deferred, was granted to this sacred lover, Our Lady, who, above all others, merits the name of "spouse" and "lover" par excellence. It was given to her by her Heavenly Spouse on the day of the Annunciation, which we celebrate today, at the same moment that this most loving sigh burst from her heart: "Let Him kiss me with the kiss of His mouth!" Then that divine union of the Eternal Word with the human nature, represented by this kiss, was made in the sacred womb of this glorious Virgin.

See how delicately this divine lover expresses her love: Let Him kiss me—that is to say: "Let this Word, which is the Word of the Father coming forth from His mouth [*Sir.* 24:3; cf. *Matt.* 4:4, *Douay*], come to unite Itself with me through the work of the Holy Spirit, who is the Eternal Sigh of the love of the Father for His Son and, reciprocally, of the Son for His Father." But when was this divine kiss given to this incomparable spouse? At the same moment that she gave this greatly desired response to the angel: "Let it be done to me as you say." [*Lk.* 1:38]. O consent worthy of great rejoicing among men, for it is the beginning of their eternal happiness! Let this be considered as a preface for what follows, for we will make a little meditation on the subsequent words which the divine lover spoke to her Beloved, by which she gave Him admirable praises.

After having first asked for this loving kiss she adds: For Your breasts are better than wine, pouring forth very sweet odors. Consider, please, how marvelously she expresses her love. The breasts of Our Lord are His loves. Your milk—or "Your loves," she means—are better than wine. In fact, the breasts represent the affections because they are placed over the heart and, as physicians say, the milk with which they are filled is as the marrow of the maternal love of mothers for their children, that love producing it for their nourishment.[2]

Now, says the dear lover: Your loves, which are Your breasts, O my Beloved, produce a certain fragrant liquor which so marvelously refreshes my soul that I have no esteem for the excellence of the most precious and delicate wines of earthly pleasures. In comparison they are nothing; they are, rather, weariness. According to Church Doctors the wine which delights and strengthens the heart [*Jgs.* 9:13; *Ps.* 104:15] represents earthly joys and satisfactions. More than all earthly pleasures, the loves of Our Lord have an incomparable strength and indescribable power to refresh the human heart—not only more than anything else, but nothing is capable of giving it perfect satisfaction except the love of God alone. Consider, if you will, all the great ones of the earth and consider their condition one after another; you will see that they are never really satisfied. If they are rich and raised to the highest dignities of this world they always desire more.

The example of Alexander, whom worldlings call "the Great," is sufficient proof of what I say. He had almost universal dominion over the whole earth. He seemed to be absolute master of it, so that the earth fell silent before him [*1 Macc.* 1:3], and princes dared not whisper a word. All trembled, so to speak, under his authority because of the great reverence they had for him. Yet having once heard a certain foolish philosopher declare that there are many worlds which he had not conquered, Alexander began to cry like a child. But for what? Alas, he said, there were so many worlds and he had not entirely conquered a single one. He was in despair at not having them all under his dominion.[3] What great foolishness!

Man takes great pleasure in trafficking in this life to find satisfaction and repose, and generally this trafficking is vain, because he derives no advantage from it. If a merchant should labor much at a certain trade which would bring him only trouble, would he not be considered very foolish and lacking in judgment? Therefore, I ask you, do not those whose understanding, being enlightened by the heavenly light, know with certainty that God alone can give true satisfaction to their hearts, carry on a very useless traffic in fixing their affections on inanimate creatures, or even on men like themselves? Worldly advantages, houses, gold and silver, riches, even honors, dignities, which our ambition makes us seek so madly—are they not vain pursuits? All these being perishable, are we not foolish to fix our hearts on them? Instead of giving true repose and tranquility, they cause eagerness and great anxiety, to preserve or increase them if we have them, or to acquire them if we do not possess them.

If we fix our love and affections on men who are living creatures capable of reason, of what profit will it be? Our traffic will still be vain since, being men like ourselves, equal in nature, they can only make us an exchange by loving us because we love them. This will be all, for not being greater than we they will be of no advantage to us and we shall receive no more than we give. We shall give them our love and they will give us theirs, one for the other. I say more: If we love the angels what shall we gain, ordinarily speaking, for they are creatures like ourselves, equally subject to God, our common Creator. Can they add anything to our stature? [*Matt.* 6:27, *Douay*]. Nothing. The cherubim and seraphim have no power to make us greater or to give us perfect satisfaction, because God has reserved that for Himself, not wishing us to fix our affections outside of Him, so jealous is He of them.

I will give you a very appropriate example on this subject. His Holiness had a singer whom he loved exceedingly, for he sang marvelously well. Although this singer was so beloved by his master, he was nevertheless inconstant, and one day he took a fancy to leave his court and go away, which he did; and his good master was much upset at his departure. Now, the Pope, devising a way to recall him, adopted this artifice. He wrote to all the princes and all the great men that if this singer should present himself they should not receive him into their service, hoping that if the poor singer found no better retreat he would return to him. It came to pass as the Pope desired, for seeing himself rejected everywhere, the singer returned to serve in the incomparable chapel of His Holiness.

The human heart is a singer infinitely loved by God, who is the Supreme Holiness, but this singer is changeable and more inconstant and fickle than can be expressed. You cannot imagine what pleasure God takes in hearing the praises that are given Him by the heart that loves Him. He delights exceedingly in the outbursts of our voices and the harmony of our music.[4] Nevertheless, this inconstant heart takes a fancy to go elsewhere, not being satisfied to please its Lord unless it pleases itself also. Intolerable folly! For what a happiness—rather, what an honor, what a favor, and what a source of perfect satisfaction to be loved by God and to dwell in the house of His Divine Majesty, that is to say, to have placed in Him all our love and to have no ambition but to be pleasing to Him! And yet this human heart allows itself to be carried away by its fancies and goes from creature to creature, from house to house, to see if it cannot find someone who will receive it and give it perfect satisfaction. But in vain, for God—who has reserved this singer for Himself alone—has commanded all creatures, of whatever nature they may be, not to give him any satisfaction or consolation whatever, that by this means he may be compelled to return to Him who is that good Master of incomparable goodness. And although this singer returns more frequently by force than by love, instead of reproaching him God does not fail to receive him and give him the same office in His chapel as before—or, it seems, even a higher one.

Oh, how great is the goodness of our God! Therefore the spouse rightly exclaims: O my Beloved, better are Your breasts beyond compare; Your loves and Your delights are a thousand times more pleasing than those of earth, for creatures, were they the highest and the most exalted, and even angels, were they brothers or sisters, could not satisfy or content us.

God has placed in our power the acquisition of His pure love which can exalt us infinitely above ourselves. He gives it to whosoever gives Him his. Why, then, do we amuse ourselves with creatures, hoping for something in the traffic that we carry on in seeking their affections?

Oh, how fully did this holy lover, Our Lady and Mistress, enjoy the sweetness of these divine breasts when, in the abundance of the consolations which she received in contemplation, transported with gladness and inexpressible happiness, she began to praise them! Oh, by her example she invites us to lay aside all desires for the satisfactions of earth, that we may have the honor and grace of drawing from them and receiving the milk of mercy, which distills drop by drop upon those who approach them to receive it.

But the spouse does not stop here for, continuing, she says that the Name of her Beloved is as an oil poured out, composed of many excellent odors which cannot be imagined, wishing to signify: My Beloved is not only perfumed, but He is perfume itself;[5] that is why, she adds, the young maidens love You.

What does the divine lover wish us to understand by these young maidens? Here young maidens represent certain young souls who, having not yet given their love anywhere, are marvelously suited to love the Heavenly Lover of our hearts, Our Lord Jesus Christ.[6] I do not mean to say, however, that if those who have given their hearts to someone withdraw them to consecrate them to God, this Sacred Spouse will not receive them heartily and accept this gift of their affections. But nevertheless He is greatly pleased with these young souls who dedicate themselves entirely to the perfection of His love. Your Name, continues the holy spouse, pours forth such delicate odors that the

young maidens love You, dedicating to You all their love
and all their affection. Oh God! What a grace to reserve all
your love for Him who recompenses us so well by giving us
His! In giving our love to creatures we receive no advantage because they return us no more than we give. But our
divine Saviour gives us His love which is as a precious
balm which diffuses a sovereign fragrance through all the
faculties of our soul.

Oh, how supremely did this young maiden, Our Lady,
love the Divine Spouse! And how supremely was she loved
by Him, for at the same time that she gave herself to Him
and consecrated her heart to Him—which was when she
pronounced these words: I am the servant of the Lord; let
it be done to me as you say, or as it will please Him[7]—immediately He descended into her chaste womb and became
the Son of her who called herself His servant. Now I know
very well that no one can ever attain to so high a degree of
perfection as to dedicate her love to God and her submission to His divine will as absolutely as Our Lady. But we
ought to desire it and to begin to do so as soon and as perfectly as possible according to our capacity, which is incomparably less than that of this holy Virgin. She is that
unique maiden who loved the Divine Spouse more excellently than any creature ever did or will do; for she
began to love Him from the moment of her glorious Conception in the womb of the good St. Anne, giving herself to
God and dedicating her love to Him as soon as she began
to exist.

The sacred spouse, continuing the conversation with her
Divine Spouse, said: Draw me, and we will run. The holy
Fathers pause to consider what this spouse means by these
words: Draw me and we will run, for it is as if she said:
"Although You draw only me, we shall be many who will
run." Some think that when she asks her Beloved to draw
her, she thus protests that she needs to be assisted by His
prevenient grace, without which we can do nothing;[8] but
when she adds: "We will run," that means: "You and I, my

Beloved, will run together." Or as some others think:
"Many will run with me in imitation of me, following me;
many souls will run after You to the odor of Your ointments."[9]

We come now to the other part of our exhortation,
which is the Profession, and the dedication which young
ladies make of their hearts to the Divine Majesty, a dedication and offering which they would never have had the
desire to make if the Sovereign Spouse of our souls had not
drawn them and assisted them with His grace. Likewise,
without the aid of this divine grace and the Constitutions
which are observed here under the guidance of our sacred
Mother and Mistress, the holy Virgin, they would never
have attained to this high rank of spouses of Jesus Christ.
Oh, happy are the religious who live in the congregation of
this divine Abbess and are instructed by this great Doctor,
who drew her knowledge from the very Heart of her dear
Son, our Saviour, who is the Wisdom of the Eternal Father.
[*Sir.* 1:4].

We shall make our third consideration on this point:[10]
that Our Lady was alone in her room when the angel came
to salute her and bring her the blessed and gracious tidings
of the Incarnation of the Word of God in her holy and
chaste womb. What do religious do but remain in their
cells and, not satisfied with that, withdraw into themselves
to remain more alone and thus render themselves more
capable of enjoying the conversation of their Spouse? They
retire into the depths of their hearts as into a heavenly
cabinet where they live in solitude. But in vain do you hide
yourselves; the angels will know well how to find you. Do
you not see that Our Lady, being all alone, was yet found
by the angel Gabriel?

Virgins and religious are never better pleased than when
they are all alone to contemplate at leisure the beauty of
their Heavenly Lover. They withdraw within themselves
because all their care is in this interior beauty, and to
preserve and increase it they are ever attentive to remove

anything which could tarnish or disfigure it in the slightest degree. The beauty of the Daughter of Sion is within, says the Psalmist [*Ps.* 44:14, *Douay*], because she knows well that the Divine Spouse beholds only her interior, while men see only the exterior. [*1 Sam.* 16:7; *Ps.* 7:10]. Now this beloved spouse is the soul who consecrates herself to follow His divine loves and who desires to please only Him; therefore she withdraws entirely into herself to prepare for Him an agreeable dwelling place. Thus in religion the exercise of the presence of God is so highly recommended and is of incomparable help. We see the proof of this in the fact that Our Lady, when practicing it and remaining recollected, merited at the same time to be chosen to be Mother of God.

This sacred Virgin was, then, a very perfect religious, as we have said, and she is the special Protectress of souls who dedicate themselves to Our Lord. But let us consider a little the virtues which she practiced and manifested more excellently than all others on the day of her glorious Annunciation, virtues which I will only mention in passing and then I will conclude. First, a virginity and purity which has nothing like it in all creation. Secondly, a sovereign and profound humility, joined and united inseparably to charity.

Virginity and absolute chastity is an angelic virtue; but though it belongs more especially to angels than to men, yet the purity of Our Lady infinitely surpassed that of the angels, having three great perfections above theirs, even that of the cherubim and seraphim. I will touch on only those three points, leaving the rest to the considerations which each of you will make in private during this octave.

The purity and virginity of Our Lady had this excellence, this privilege and supereminence above that of the angels, that it was a fruitful virginity. That of the angels is sterile and can produce no fruit. On the contrary, that of our glorious Mistress was not only fruitful because she produced for us this sweet Fruit of Life, Our Lord and

Master, but in the second place she has begotten many virgins. It is in imitation of her, as we have said, that virgins have vowed their chastity. But the virginity of this divine Mother has also the property of restoring and repairing those who had been stained and defiled at some period of their life. Holy Scripture testifies that during her lifetime she called a great number of virgins, so that many accompanied her wherever she went: St. Martha, St. Marcella, the Marys, and many others. [Cf. *Lk.* 8:2-3; *Jn.* 19:25; *Acts* 1:14]. But in particular, was it not by means of her and by her example that St. Mary Magdalene, who was a cauldron blackened by a thousand impurities and the receptacle of impurity itself, was afterwards enrolled under the standard of the purity of Our Lady and converted into a crystal vial, resplendent and transparent, capable of receiving and retaining the most precious liquors and most salutary waters?

Therefore the virginity of our divine Mistress is not sterile like that of the angels, but is so fruitful that from the moment it was vowed to God until the present time, it has always brought forth new fruit. And not only is it fruitful itself, but it also begets a fruitful virginity in others; for a soul who dedicates herself perfectly to the divine service will never be alone, but will draw many after her example to follow the "perfumes" which have attracted her. Therefore the sacred lover says to her Beloved: Draw me, and we will run.

Moreover, the virginity of Our Lady surpassed that of the angels because they are virgins and chaste by nature. It is not customary to praise a person for what he has naturally because, being without choice, that does not merit praise. We do not praise the sun because it is luminous, for this property being natural to it, it cannot cease to shine. The angels are in no way praiseworthy because they are virgins and chaste, for they cannot be otherwise. But our sacred Mistress has a virginity worthy to be exalted because it is chosen, elected, and vowed. Although she was married, it was not to the prejudice of her virginity, because her husband was a virgin, and like her had vowed to remain so always. Oh, how dearly did this holy Lady love this virtue. Therefore she bound herself to it by vow. She is always accompanied by virgins and she favors them in a special manner.

Her virginity also surpassed that of the angels because it was tried and tested, which could not be the case with that of the heavenly spirits, for they could not fall from their purity nor receive any attack or trial whatsoever. Our glorious Father, St. Augustine, speaking to the angels, says: It is not difficult for you, O blessed spirits, to be virgins, since you are not and cannot be tempted.

Some may think it strange if I say that the purity of Our Lady was tried and tested, but this is true; she was tested with a very great trial. God forbid that we should think that this trial resembled ours, for being all pure and purity itself, she could not receive the attacks to which we are subject and which torment us who bear temptation within us. These temptations would not have dared to approach the impregnable walls of her integrity. They are so importunate that the great Apostle St. Paul writes that three times he besought Our Lord to take them away, or else to moderate their violence so that he could resist them without offense and without yielding. [*2 Cor.* 12:7-8].

The sacred Virgin was tested when she saw the angel in human form. Do we not notice that she began to fear and be troubled, so that St. Gabriel, knowing it, said to her: "Do not fear, Mary" [*Lk.* 1:29-30]; for he meant to say: Although you see me in the form of a man, I am not a man, nor do I wish to speak to you from a human perspective. He said this because he noticed that the virginal modesty of Our Lady was disturbed. A holy man writes that modesty is, as it were, the sacristan of chastity. As the sacristan of a church is very careful to lock the doors lest its altars should be robbed, and always looks about to see if anything has been stolen, so the modesty of virgins is always on the watch to see that nothing comes to attack their chastity or endanger their virginity, of which they are extremely jealous; and as soon as they perceive anything questionable, though it should be only the shadow of evil, they are troubled as was the august Mary.

But she was not only virgin par excellence above all others, angels as well as men—she was also more humble than all others. This was manifest excellently on the day of the Annunciation. She then made the greatest act of humility that was ever made or ever will be made by a pure creature; for seeing herself exalted by the angel who saluted her, saying that she was full of grace and that she would conceive a Son who would be both God and man, she was troubled and began to fear. [*Lk.* 1:28-32]. Certainly she was familiar with angels, but she had never before been praised by them, for it is not their custom to praise anyone except sometimes for encouragement in some great undertaking. [*Jgs.* 6:12,14]. Therefore, hearing holy Gabriel offer her such extraordinary praise, she was anxious, thereby teaching maidens who take pleasure in being flattered that they expose themselves to great danger of receiving some blemish to their virginity and purity; for humility is so truly the companion of virginity that virginity will never remain long in the soul that has no humility. Although one may be found without the other, as is often seen in the world where many married persons live humbly, yet it must be confessed that these two virtues cannot exist, one without the other, in virgins, that is, in maidens.

Our Lady, being reassured by the angel and having learned what God willed to do with her and in her, made this supreme act of humility, saying: I am the servant of the Lord. Let it be done to me as you say. She saw herself raised to the highest dignity that ever was or will be, for though it should please God to create anew many worlds, He could never make a pure creature be greater than the Mother of God. This dignity is incomparable; and yet the sacred Virgin is not puffed up, but declares that she will always remain the servant of the Divine Majesty. And to show that she was so and willed to be so, she said: Let it be done to me, all according to His good pleasure—abandoning herself to the mercy of His divine will, protesting that by her own choice and election she will always remain in lowliness, and will preserve humility as the inseparable companion of virginity.

But if these two virtues, humility and virginity, may be found one without the other, this separation cannot exist between humility and charity. They are indivisible, and so joined and united together that one is never found without the other, if they are true and unfeigned. When the activity of the one ceases, it is followed immediately by the activity of the other; as soon as humility has abased itself, charity raises itself up toward Heaven.[11] These two virtues are like Jacob's ladder, upon which the angels were going up and coming down. [*Gen.* 28:12-13]. This does not mean that of themselves they could ascend and descend at the same time; these angels did not do this, for they ascended in order to descend again. Humility would seem to remove us from God, who abides at the top of the ladder, because it always makes us descend, in order to lower, despise, and abase ourselves; nevertheless, it is quite the contrary, for in proportion as we abase ourselves, we render ourselves more capable of ascending to the top of this ladder where we shall meet the Eternal Father.

Our Lady humbled herself and acknowledged herself unworthy of being raised to the high dignity of Mother of God; therefore she was made to be His Mother, for she had no sooner uttered the protestation of her littleness than, having abandoned herself to Him by an act of incomparable charity, she became the Mother of the Most High, who is the Saviour of our souls.

If we act thus, my dear daughters, and unite virginity with humility, immediately accompanying it with most holy charity, which will raise us to the top of Jacob's mystical ladder, we shall certainly be received into the bosom of the

Eternal Father, who will cover us with a thousand heavenly consolations. Then, in the enjoyment of these we will sing, after Our Lady and most holy Mistress, the canticle of praise to this God who has given us so much grace to follow Him in this world and to combat under His standard. Amen.

Addition[12]

When the divine lover says: "Draw me," she assures us we cannot do anything without grace, for she immediately adds: "We will run." [*Song* 1:4].

The most holy Virgin alone was the first to be drawn by the Heavenly Spouse to consecrate and dedicate herself totally to His service. For she was the first to consecrate her body and soul to God by the vow of virginity. But as soon as she was drawn she drew a host of souls who offered themselves to God, to advance under her sacred protection in the observance of a perfect and inviolable virginity and chastity. Ever since she led the way it has always been filled with souls who come to consecrate themselves, by vows, to the service of the Divine Majesty. Most dear souls, whom the glorious Virgin regards when she says: "We will run"! Thereby she assures her Beloved that many will follow her standard, striving under her authority against all kinds of enemies for the glory of His Name. [*Ps.* 79:9].

O what an honor for us to do battle under this valiant captainess! Women seem to have a particular obligation to follow this courageous warrior, who has so infinitely ennobled and honored them.[13] Oh! If God's Mother had an angelic nature, how the cherubim and seraphim should glory in it and consider themselves honored! Our Lady is indeed the honor, prototype, and patron of men and of women who live virtuously and of widows. However, no one can deny that young girls, more than all others, have a certain more particular alliance with her. Their similarity to her virginity, belonging to their sex and condition, gives them a great capacity and advantage in approaching her more closely.

As for myself, I think the reason for making, during all ages, a greater solemnity of their entrance and Profession in religion than that of men is this: Their sex being more fragile, their very courageous act of entering religion should be all the more honored. Also, on these feasts God is pleased to be more honored than in the Profession which men make of living in religion. To tell the truth, men do not make so great a renouncement of their liberty as do women. These latter enclose themselves in celestial prisons of Our Lord—the religious orders—to pass the rest of their days. They are never permitted to go abroad except for certain very rare and special occasions, as to found and establish monasteries.

Men entering religion intend, indeed, to live in obedience according to its Rules and statutes. But, it must be confessed, the renouncement they make of their liberty is not so extreme as that of women. Men still have the freedom to go out, to go from convent to convent, to preach, to hear confessions, and to perform many other exercises of their ministry, which are really diversions for them. They, indeed, leave the world in affection, for all religious ought to do this. Nevertheless, they always have some contact with persons in the world, and this relieves somewhat the rigorous law of monastic enclosure.

When young girls dedicate themselves to God they reject and abandon all that. They renounce even the very thing to which nature clings most tenaciously, their liberty. Thus, it can well be said that these young girls perform an act above nature, and need God's supernatural strength to make so perfect an act as that of dedicating themselves to His divine service by such a complete renouncement. For we do not deceive them, telling them that in religion Our Lord will give them sugar, like children, to coax them. Nor are they told that they will be led to Mount Thabor where they will say with St. Peter: "How good that we are here!" [*Matt.* 17:4]. On the contrary, they are warned before the novitiate and Profession: You must go to "Mount Calvary," where, with Our Lord, you must be "crucified." You must crucify your understanding, restraining all your thoughts, not admitting any voluntarily but those consonant with your chosen vocation. You must likewise crucify your memory, never dwelling upon any remembrance of what you have left in the world. Finally, you must crucify and attach your own will to the Cross of Our Lord, never using it for your own pleasure, but living in perfect submission and obedience for the rest of your life.

Tell me, please, having represented to young girls only the cross, thorns, lances, nails and, finally, the mortifications of the religious life, is not this a very considerable act which they make, and worthy to be honored? O extremely generous souls who truly manifest that you do battle and advance under the auspices of our holy and glorious Mistress, the most holy Virgin! Oh, doubtless, these young women must have considered that it is the property of love to render the burden light; the bitter, sweet; and the insupportably difficult, easy. Your glorious Father St. Augustine[14] expressed this truth very well, saying[15] that he who loves finds nothing vexatious, unpleasant or too troublesome. "There is no toil," he says, "where there is love, or if there is, it is loved."

Go then, my dear daughters, or rather, come with love to dedicate yourselves to God and to the service of His most pure love. Although you will meet with trials you will love this trouble, being well assured that you will please God and render yourselves acceptable to your dear Patroness who, though she had not the name of religious, nevertheless practiced the exercises of religion. Although she is the Protectress of all people and each vocation in general, she has made herself nevertheless Protectress in a special way of virgins who are dedicated to the service of her Son in religion, seeing that she has been like an abbess who showed by example all that they must do to live religiously. For your consideration I shall touch upon only three points concerning today's Gospel to prove what I say. It tells us that, in addressing himself to this holy Virgin to announce the incomparable Mystery of the Incarnation of the Eternal Word, the angel found her retired and alone in her room, in Galilee, in the city of Nazareth. [*Lk.* 1:26-38].

As to the first point: Our Lady was in the country of Galilee. "Galilee" is a Hebrew word meaning "migration." You know there are two kinds of birds: birds of passage or migrating birds, and those that are not. The former migrate because they go from one country to another, like the swallows and nightingales, which ordinarily are found in these parts only in spring and summer. In winter they migrate, withdrawing to countries where it is spring and warm weather when the cold of winter is here. When our springtime returns they return and once again migrate, that is, pass from one country to another, coming here to recreate us with their pleasant warblings.

Are not religious, men and women, in a country of migration? Do they not make a passage from the world into religion, as into a place of springtime, to chant the divine praises, and to avoid the bitter cold of the world? Oh! Is it not for this that they enter religion where it is always springtime and warm, the Sun of Justice [*Mal.* 3:20] most usually darting His rays upon religious hearts—not warming less in enlightening them than He enlightens in warming them? What is the world but an extremely cold winter where there are only frozen and icy souls? I mean those in the world and of the world, for I know well enough that one can live perfectly in any kind of vocation, in the world as well as in religion, and provided one is so resolved, one can attain a high degree of perfection anywhere. But ordinarily speaking, in the world one almost always meets only icy hearts. They are so cold and so slightly warmed by this Supreme Fire from which all other fires draw their origin and their heat! As it is the sun that gives heat to everything on earth, yes, even to fire which without it could not produce heat,[16] so the love of God is this Sun which gives heat to the human heart when it is disposed to receive it. Without this Sacred Fire it would remain unspeakably cold.

Our Lady, then, like religious, was in a country of migration. But, O God! How admirably well she made this migration, passing from one degree of perfection to a higher. Briefly, her life was nothing else but a continual passage from virtue to virtue. [*Ps.* 84:6,8]. In this all religious ought to imitate her as perfectly as they can, since they are the ones who are closer to her than all others. For doubtless, they are those virgins of whom the Psalmist says: Behind her the virgins of her train are brought to the King. [*Ps.* 45:15]. Love never says: "Enough, sufficient." It desires to have the courage always to progress on the way of the will of the Beloved.

My second remark upon the Gospel is this: Our Lady was found by the angel in the city of Nazareth. Now, "Nazareth" means "flower." She was then in the city of flowers—or flowery city. Oh, how well this city represents religion! For what is religion but a flowering city, or a house all strewn with flowers, since the Rules and statutes which religious observe are as so many flowers? Mortifications, humiliations, prayers—in short, all the exercises are nothing else than the practice of virtues which are like beautiful flowers shedding their exceedingly sweet perfume before the Divine Majesty. Now what is religion but a garden sown with flowers, very pleasing to the sight, and with fragrance very healthful to the scent of those who notice them?

So it is said of the most holy Virgin that she was in a flowery city. What is she herself but a flower chosen from among all others for her rare beauty and excellence? A flower which, because of its incomparably sweet fragrance, has the property of engendering and producing other flowers. And do you not know that she is that garden, enclosed and shut tight in the Song of Songs, all empearled and enamelled? [*Song* 4:12]. An enclosed garden, my sister, my bride, an enclosed garden. This repetition is not without mystery. To whom belong, I ask you, so many flowers with which the Church is filled and so embellished and adorned, if not to the most holy Virgin, whose example produced them all? Is it not through her that the Church is strewn with the roses of martyrs, invincible in their constancy; marigolds of so many holy confessors; violets of so many holy widows who are little, humble, lowly like these flowers, but who spread abroad a good and fragrant perfume? Finally, is it not to her that in a special way belong so many white lilies, so many pure souls, and so many virgins so innocent and guileless, since it has been to imitate her example that so many virgins have consecrated their hearts and bodies to the Divine Majesty by a determination and an indissoluble vow to preserve their virginity and purity.

There are some Doctors who hold that she instituted congregations of young girls, and that when she went to Ephesus with her dear adopted son, St. John, she founded one to which she herself gave Rules and Constitutions. Oh, what a divine Abbess! Oh, what happy religious to have been established by this divine Doctor![17]

NOTES

1. The Blessed Virgin Mary. Cf. also note 2, p. 23.
2. Cf. *Treatise,* Bk. 5, ch. 2.
3. Cf. *Treatise,* Bk. 3, ch. 10.
4. Cf. *Treatise,* Bk. 9, ch. 9.
5. Cf. *Treatise,* Bk. 5, ch. 11; Sermon for Nov. 21, 1617, p. 35-36.
6. Cf. *Treatise,* Bk. 10, ch. 4-5.
7. Cf. above, p. 135-136.
8. Cf. *Treatise,* Bk. 2, ch. 13, 21; *Conferences,* I; Sermon for Nov. 21, 1617, p. 43-44.

9. Cf. *Treatise,* Bk. 7, ch. 2.
10. The second point which St. Francis de Sales developed is missing from the original manuscripts.
11. Cf. *Conferences,* VIII, p. 136.
12. As was noted above, St. Francis' second point is missing from the original manuscripts. The editor of the 1641 edition of his works added this fragment from another of St. Francis' sermons. The editor of the Annecy edition, from which this translation is made, kept this addition. We are doing the same.—Ed.
13. Cf. Sermon for Sept. 10, 1620, p. 101.
14. Cf. Sermon for Sept. 10, 1620, p. 115, note 10.
15. Cf. *Treatise,* Bk. 8, ch. 5.
16. Cf. *Treatise,* Bk. 7, ch. 5.
17. The fragment ends here, somewhat abruptly.

— 11 —

THE VISITATION

Sermon for the Feast of the Visitation, July 2, 1621, concerning the admirable unions of contraries effected by God, especially the union of charity and humility as practiced by Our Lady at the Annunciation and Visitation, the pride and frivolity of human beings (especially of women), St. Elizabeth's reception of the Holy Spirit at the Visitation and what this teaches us about our reception of the Holy Spirit, our relationship to the angels and saints and what we should ask them for, and the visits of Our Lady to us and in what way we should desire and respond to them.

God, who is One, loves unity and union; and all that is not unified is displeasing to Him, as the great Apostle Paul says: One Lord, one faith, one baptism, one God and Father of all.[1] [*Gal.* 3:20; *Eph.* 4:5-6]. But if He sovereignly loves what is united and conjoined, He is the enemy of disunion, for what is disunited is imperfect, disunion being caused only by imperfection. Being the Master and Lover of union, then, Our Lord has established three admirable unions in the sacred Virgin Our Lady, exclusive of the natural union of soul and body.

Now this natural union of soul and body is so excellent that all the philosophers have not yet exhausted nor defined their admiration of it, seeing that God has conjoined soul and body with so strict a joining that the body, without ceasing to be body, and the spirit, without ceasing to be spirit, form nevertheless only one person. This natural union is so exalted that we cannot give it the admiration due to it; indeed, it is the work of a God most high and a Lover of unity.

But it is not of this natural union of soul and body in Our Lady that I wish to speak, inasmuch as it is universal and common to the rest of humankind; I wish to dwell on three other admirable unions which God effected in her. The first is that of the Divine Nature with human nature in her sacred womb, which is so elevated a mystery that it infinitely surpasses all that human and angelic understandings can conceive or comprehend. Never would the thought of so admirable a union have dared to enter the mind of any angel, cherubim or seraphim, for these two natures, the Divine and human, are so far removed from each other, and there is so great a distance between them, that no angelic creature could have thought that God had willed to effect this union. Divine Nature is the highest, and human nature is the lowest; Divine Nature is sovereign perfection, while human nature is sovereign misery. They are then two extremes, two great opposites; nevertheless, God has effected so admirable a conjoining of these two natures in the womb of the Virgin that they constitute only one Person, so that man is God, and God, without ceasing to be God, is man.

The second union which He effected in Our Lady was that of maternity with virginity, a union which is absolutely outside the course of nature, for it unites two things which it is impossible to find together in nature. Indeed, never was there seen nor did the thought exist that a mother was virgin, and that a virgin, without ceasing to be virgin, was mother. It is, then, a miraculous and supernatural union, effected by the all-powerful hand of God, who gave this privilege to our glorious Mistress; and as this union has happened in her alone, so will she alone remain ever Virgin and Mother at the same time.

The third union is that of a very exalted charity and a

very profound humility. The union of these two virtues is certainly admirable inasmuch as they are greatly removed from each other, so that it seems that they could never meet in one same soul. Charity elevates the soul on high, and the more it increases and is perfected, the more also it exalts and elevates the soul in which it dwells. Humility does just the contrary: It abases the soul in its own esteem and in the esteem of all creatures, having for its proper effect that the greater the humility, the more it lowers in its own eyes the soul in which it dwells.[2] You see a little of the opposition between these two virtues and you say: How can we harmonize, unite and join together humility and charity since the nature of one is to ascend on high and that of the other to descend downward? It is impossible on the natural plane.

It is true that none but God could effect the union of these two virtues; but He who is one sole God wills and loves unity, and delights in displaying the greatness of His power by bringing about these admirable unions. Now, He has united charity and humility in the holy Virgin in such wise that there could be no charity in her without humility nor humility without charity; charity remaining humble and humility charitable; charity exalting the soul above all creatures and above itself, and humility abasing it below all—these two virtues remaining nevertheless conjoined in such wise that one cannot subsist without the other.

It is on this last union that I will dwell, which will lead me into the subject of this feast; for what is the Visitation of Our Lady to holy Elizabeth if not a meeting of humility and charity, or a summary of the effects of these two virtues practiced by the holy Virgin toward her cousin?[3] Humility and charity have only one object, God, as they tend toward union with Him; nevertheless they pass from God to the neighbor, and it is in this transfer that they attain their perfection. Certainly our most glorious Mistress practiced these two virtues in a sovereign degree at the time of the Incarnation[4] when, the Angel Gabriel having announced this ineffable Mystery to her, she responded: I am the servant of the Lord; let it be done to me as you say. [*Lk.* 1:38]. For while he was declaring her Mother of God and Queen of angels and men, while he was giving her to understand that she was to be exalted above all creatures angelic and human, she was lowering herself at the feet of all, saying: I am the chambermaid of the Lord. Great humility this! The holy Virgin had then such a clear knowledge of the misery of our nature and the distance between God and man that, seeing herself exalted and chosen above all, she abased herself to the lowest depths of her nothingness before the incomprehensible and inexhaustible abyss of the immense goodness of God.

It is true that she never humbled herself so profoundly as when she said: I am the servant of the Lord. But after having made acts of so perfect a humility and self-annihilation and having abased herself as low as she could, she immediately brought forth acts of charity, adding: Let it be done to me as you say. For in giving her consent and acquiescence to what the angel announced that God had asked of her, she demonstrated the greatest charity conceivable. You see then how at this moment God united charity and humility in the holy Virgin. In saying: I am the servant of the Lord, she abased herself to the profound abyss of her nothingness, but at the same time she was raised above the cherubim and seraphim by her charity when she added: Let it be done to me as you say. For at that moment the Divine Word took flesh in her virginal womb, and by this means she became Mother of God.

Behold how humility is joined to charity in Our Lady and how her humility exalts her; for God looks upon the lowly to raise them up [*Ps.* 113:7; 138:6]; that is why, seeing this holy Virgin humble herself beneath all creatures, He casts His eyes upon her and exalts her above all. This is what she herself makes us understand by the words of her sacred canticle [*Lk.* 1:48]: Because the Lord has looked upon my abjection, my lowliness and my misery, all nations shall call me blessed.[5] It is as if she had meant to say to St. Elizabeth: You proclaim me blessed [*Lk.* 1:45], and it is true that I am, but all my happiness proceeds from the fact that God has looked upon my abjection and my lowliness.

However, Our Lady was not satisfied with having thus humbled herself before the Divine Majesty, for she well knew that humility and charity are not in their perfection until they are transmitted to the neighbor. From the love of God proceeds love of the neighbor; and the great Apostle says: The greatness of your love for your brothers will be directly proportioned to the greatness of your love for God. [Cf. *Rom.* 13:8; *Gal.* 5:14; *Eph.* 5:1-2]. St. John teaches us this when he writes: How can it be that you love God, whom you do not see, if you do not love your neighbor, whom you do see? [*1 Jn.* 4:20].

If then we wish to prove that we do indeed love God, and if we wish others to believe us when we assure them of this, we must love our brothers well, serve them and assist them in their necessities. Now the holy Virgin, knowing this truth, set out promptly, says the Evangelist, proceeding in haste into the hill country of Judah [*Lk.* 1:39], into the town of Hebron, or, as others say, Jerusalem (it matters little), to serve her cousin Elizabeth in her advanced age and pregnancy. In this she manifested great humility and charity; for as soon as she saw herself Mother of God, she humbled herself to the point of immediately setting out on the road to go help and assist that good woman. It may not have been at that very hour, nor even on the very same day that she learned it, for I leave it to you to think that this holy Virgin remained in her little home, recollected and ravished in awesome wonder, meditating on this profound and incomprehensible Mystery that had been wrought in her. O God, what sweetness and delight did she not feel in her heart from the knowledge of this marvel! Oh, how many holy conversations and loving colloquies between the Son and the Mother!

She did not then leave on the very day of the Incarnation, but some days later, and proceeded in haste into the hill country of Juda. But what humility this! She goes to become the chambermaid and servant of her who was in everything and in every way inferior to her; for although St. Elizabeth was of noble extraction since she was of the tribe of Levi, being married to a high priest [*Lk.* 1:5], and on the maternal side she belonged to the house of David, yet for all that she was as nothing compared to the Virgin. Our Lady is Queen of Heaven and of earth, of angels and of men; yet these titles that we give her serve only to assist our poor understandings to picture her to ourselves in some fashion that we might comprehend her greatness a little, since she is sovereignly greater than all we can say of her. If we wish to give her a name worthy of her excellence, we must name her Mother of God;[6] for this word is so exalted that all the titles, praises, and commendations we could give her are contained in it.

What humility, then, is that of the holy Virgin, when she has been chosen and declared Mother of the Eternal Word; she calls herself the servant of the Lord, and, as a chambermaid, sets out on her way to serve that good Elizabeth in her advanced years. O my God! How great and profound was that humility which she demonstrated in greeting her cousin, for the Evangelist notes that Our Lady, as the more humble, was the first to offer the greeting. [*Lk.* 1:40].

But what blessings and graces entered this home with the sacred Virgin! We know this from the words of St. Elizabeth who, in a spirit of prophecy, cried out in a voice clear and distinct: But who am I that the Mother of my Lord should come to me? Then continuing, she said: Blest is she who trusted that the Lord's words to her would be fulfilled. Blest are you among women, and blest is the Fruit of your womb, Jesus. Yes, this Fruit is not only blest but it is He who gives all blessings; and your coming has brought me so much happiness and consolation that the baby leapt in my womb for joy. [*Lk.* 1:42-45].

O God! Who can imagine the sweetness and delights that flowed into the heart of St. Elizabeth at this Visitation? How she pondered this great Mystery of the Incarnation and the graces and favors that the Lord had granted her! What loving words, what divine conversations were held between St. John in his mother's womb with his dear Master whom he knew and adored in the womb of Our Lady! What blessings and enlightenments this dear Saviour of our souls poured forth into the heart of His forerunner! At that moment He bestowed upon him the use of reason; but I will not speak of that at the present because I remember well having spoken to you about it on former occasions.[7]

I will touch upon only these two or three points with you in passing, to console and comfort your spirits. The first is that St. John had the use of reason; the second, that he was sanctified in his mother's womb; and the third, that he was filled with wisdom and the knowledge of God and divine mysteries and therefore he loved Him, adored Him, and leapt for joy. While yet in their mothers' wombs, Our Lord and St. John the Baptist knew each other, conversed together, and loved each other, having the use of affection, judgment and reason. The rest of us are indeed alive in the maternal womb, but we do not yet have the use of our faculties; we are there as a mass of flesh, and although we have our senses, still we cannot make use of them. St. John must have recognized the Saviour in the womb of Our Lady, since at His arrival he leapt for joy in his mother's womb; he must also have loved Him, for we do not leap for joy over the coming of those we neither know nor love. Now St. Elizabeth gave testimony to this truth by the words she spoke to the Virgin.

But what did Our Lady do amidst all these praises and benedictions? She did not react as women of the world who, if they are extolled, instead of humbling themselves exalt themselves the more. Man is so subject to pride and presumption that we can apply to him what Aristotle, that ancient philosopher, says of the horse—namely, that there is nothing so haughty. Indeed, if you watch a horse, do you not see his pride in his mane, his head, his whole bearing? He strikes the cobblestones impatiently and makes sparks fly with his hooves. Likewise, see some young dandy, some young fool; do you not mark his pride, his presumption and vanity? Notice his gait, his bearing, how he struts and carries his head high; in short, he exhibits a thousand follies and pompous gestures which are all marks of his pride and overweening conceit. Now consider a man on horseback: We do not know which is the more haughty, the horse or its rider; it seems as if they compete with each other in displaying their vanity.

Certainly, man is greatly subject to this pride and presumption, but when this vice enters the heads of women it produces even greater ruin and destruction; and because women are so subject to the desire of making a good impression on others, they are constrained to give particular attention to guarding and preserving this impression. The weakness of their sex leads them to this: The slightest thing arouses their vanity; oftentimes they fabricate thoughts and opinions of themselves which make them think themselves far superior to others. This ordinarily happens to weak minds; and the more imperfect they are, the more subject to such foibles, foolishness and pomposity. We have an example of this in that senseless, foolish and impudent Cleopatra. What impertinences and extravagances did she not resort to in order to glorify herself![8] And Eve, the first woman, on merely being told that she was created to the image of God, became so presumptuous that she wished to make herself like Him; with this end in view, she listened to and did all that the enemy suggested to her. [*Gen.* 1:27; 3:5-6].

But the sacred Virgin came to regain by her humility what the first Eve had lost by her pride; thus, she reversed Eve's pride and presumption by her humility. When the angel calls her Mother of God, she, plunging herself into the abyss of her nothingness, calls herself His chamber-maid; and when Elizabeth proclaims her blest among women, she replies that this blessing arises from the fact that the Lord had looked upon her lowliness, her littleness, her abjection. O God, what a good sign in the spiritual life is humility of heart! It is a good indication that we have received divine graces efficaciously when these graces abase and humble us, and we see that the greater these graces are, so much the more do they profoundly annihilate the heart before God and creatures; so that, like the holy Virgin, we find all our happiness in the realization that the eyes of the Divine Goodness have looked upon our poverty and misery!

Profound humility and ardent charity, as much toward God as toward the neighbor, are thus the fruits produced in Our Lady's heart by the grace of God. Charity made her go in haste to the home of Zechariah, for although she was pregnant, her Divine Child was not burdensome to her, so that she experienced no encumbrance on the way. As she had conceived Him by the overshadowing of the Holy Spirit [*Lk.* 1:35], she carried Him without inconvenience and brought Him forth without pain—Our Lord reserving her pangs of childbirth for the day of His Crucifixion, which His holy Mother must witness.

Thus, this incomparable Virgin enters Zechariah's house, and with her a superabundance of blessings for this family; for, as the Evangelist says, St. John the Baptist was sanctified in his mother's womb and St. Elizabeth was filled with the Holy Spirit. [*Lk.* 1:41]. I know well that Elizabeth was a holy lady who already had the Holy Spirit in her. Then how are we to understand that she received Him at the coming of the Virgin? There can be no doubt that she did receive Him then, for the admirable effects that He brought about in her furnish sufficient proof of it. God gives His grace to the just in good measure, pressed down, shaken together, running over. [*Lk.* 6:38]. Now, although Elizabeth had a good measure of the grace of the Holy

Spirit, nevertheless at the Visitation of the Virgin she received it pressed down, shaken together and running over, since during this life grace is given in such a way that there can always be an increase and growth in its communication.[9] We must, then, be careful never to say: It is enough, I have a sufficiency of divine grace or virtues; enough of mortification, I have exercised myself sufficiently in that area.

That would be a serious error; and he who would speak such or similar words would thereby demonstrate his indigence, his destitution and the poverty that stalks him [*Rev.* 3:17]; for from such persons who think they have a sufficiency, God takes away what they have. "To the man who has, more will be given," says Our Lord; "the man who has not, will lose what little he has." [*Matt.* 13:12; 25:29]. This should be thus understood: To the man who has received much and has labored much and who does not relax, thinking he has no more need of anything, but who with a holy and true humility knows his poverty, more will be given. To the man who has much, still more will be given; but he who has received some grace and believes he has a sufficiency will lose what little he has, and nothing more will be given him.

Worldlings have a certain ambition to acquire riches and honors and never say: "Enough!" How blind they are in this, for however little they possess would be sufficient inasmuch as too much glory, wealth and dignities cause the death and loss of our souls. Certainly in all these things we can say: I have a moderate amount, I am satisfied, I have enough; but in what concerns spiritual goods, oh! While we are in this land of exile, we must never think that we have enough of them but must continually dispose ourselves to receive an increase of grace.

Our Lady, then, went to visit St. Elizabeth; but this visit was not useless nor like those which women of the world very often make solely for ceremony, to testify the deepest affections which they do not feel, and during them they frequently gossip about each other so that they come away with guilty consciences. St. Jerome, speaking of the devout lady Proba, describes the uselessness of the visits of the Roman ladies in an admirable manner, saying that those good women did nothing but exchange visits, and that most of these were unnecessary and a waste of time, a fact he deplores in this letter. Formerly there were many prayer gatherings, and greetings by way of prayer besides the complimentary greetings as still occur among gentlemen who meet, saying: "God be with us"; "God grant you a good day, a good year"; "May God help us." The Greeks used this salutation: "May God be with us, may God bless us"; the Jewish Christian: *Pax Christi*—"May the peace of Our Lord be with you"; and among the Latins: *Laus Deo, Deo gratias*—"Glory be to God, praised be God." In our time they use more complimentary expressions and say: "Sir, I am your servant; I kiss your hand"; and ordinarily they give no thought to what they say.

Our Lady's Visitation was not like that, for she went to serve her cousin. Their conversations were far from idle— rather, my God! How holy, pious and devout! That visit filled the whole family of Zechariah with the Holy Spirit. Now, the principle effects of the Holy Spirit are those which He produced in St. Elizabeth; you can easily understand this if you have also received Him. The first thing St. Elizabeth did was to humble herself profoundly, for, seeing the Virgin, she exclaimed: But who am I that the Mother of my Lord should come to me? This is the first fruit of the grace of God, humility; when grace visits the soul, it inclines it to efface itself in the awareness of the Divine Goodness and its own nothingness and deficiency.

Secondly, Elizabeth said: O how blest is she who trusted! And then: Blest are you among women and blest is the Fruit of your womb. By this you see that the second effect of the Holy Spirit is to make us remain firm in the faith and to confirm that of others; then to return to God, acknowledging that He is the source of all graces. "It is true," St. Elizabeth seems to say to the Virgin, "that you are blest among women, but it is also true that this blessedness comes to you from the Fruit of your womb, who is the Lord of all blessedness"; for we do not bless the fruit because of the tree, but the tree because of the goodness of its fruit.

And so, though we owe the sacred Virgin a cult and honor greater than we have for all other saints, nevertheless it must not equal that which we render to God. I say this to refute the heresy of some who hold that we must honor her in the same way as Our Lord, which is false; for we must adore God alone in and above all things [*Dt.* 6:13; 10:20; *Matt.* 4:10], and then render a very special honor to Our Lady as Mother of our Saviour and cooperator in our salvation. Such is the practice of the true Christian, and anyone who does not love and honor the Virgin with a quite special and particular love is not a true Christian. Thus, when the Holy Spirit comes to us, He leads us to love and praise God, and then His most holy Mother.

In the third place Elizabeth said that her baby leapt in her womb for joy; and this is the third mark of the visit of the Holy Spirit—interior conversion, the change to a better life. St. John was sanctified; likewise whoever receives the Holy Spirit is wholly transformed in God. If, then, you wish to know if you have received Him, examine your works, for it is by them that we know the answer.

But notice that St. Elizabeth received the Holy Spirit by means of the Virgin. Certainly we must avail ourselves of her as a mediatrix with her Son in order to obtain this Divine Spirit; and although we can go directly to God and ask for His graces without employing the mediation of the saints for this purpose, nevertheless Divine Providence has not willed that it happen so; but It has formed still another union, for God is One, as I told you at the beginning, and so He loves what is unified. Therefore He has so united the Church Militant with the Church Triumphant that the two make only one, having only one Lord who rules, guides, governs and nourishes them, though in different ways; thus we address ourselves to Him to ask for our daily bread [*Matt.* 6:11; *Lk.* 11:3], as much for our bodily needs as for the nourishment required for the soul.

Consider further that the Saviour, in willing to form this union, willed and ordained that we have recourse to the invocation of the saints. He has granted great favors to people through their intercession, and at other times He has employed that of the angels. But why does He employ the mediation of angels to protect us and bestow His graces on us? Could He not do it just as well Himself without using them? Doubtless He could, but in order to realize this union of which I speak, He has determined to unite angels with men and subject them one to the other. He has willed that the latter be served by the heavenly spirits, and that through this union the conversion of men should augment the angels' glory.

But, you will say to me, how can men cause joy to the angels? Do they not have perfect happiness in the vision of God? Of this there is no doubt; nevertheless, does not Holy Scripture testify that there will be more joy in Heaven over one converted sinner than over ninety-nine righteous people? [*Lk.* 15:7,10]. By these words you see the joy of the angels over the conversion of a sinner. Now, when I say that the angels celebrate in Heaven and rejoice, we must understand the same for the saints who are with them; for though the Evangelist speaks only of the blessed spirits, it is because before the Passion of Our Lord there were not yet any people in Heaven; but since the saints have entered there, they are so united with the angels that they share in their joy over the return of sinners. That is why the Church, like a good mother, wishing the better to teach us to make use of the mediation of the holy Virgin and the saints, joined the *Ave Maria* to the *Pater* so that we should recite it immediately after the Lord's Prayer.

There is no doubt that we may ask God, through Our Lady's intercession, not only for spiritual goods such as the virtues, but also for temporal ones. However, it is also true that we should not have recourse to so great a Virgin for trifles as some do—for example, to become richer or more beautiful, and the like nonsense; for just as it would be a grave discourtesy to employ a great prince's influence with the king or emperor to obtain some trifle of small account, so in the spiritual life it would be discourteous to employ the mediation of our glorious Queen for insignificant and transitory things. Moreover, we should always treat holy things, the saints and the sacred Virgin, with profound honor and respect. Certainly, when we speak of them we should prostrate our hearts to the earth, for the distance between us and these heavenly spirits is unimaginable; nevertheless, the affinity is so great that just as the earth is incapable of producing anything without the cooperation of the heavens, in like manner neither can we do anything of ourselves if we are not assisted by the saints. But we must avail ourselves of their assistance in what benefits us for eternity, beseeching them to obtain the grace of God and the virtues for us, employing the credit they have with our dear Saviour and Master for these gifts and others like them, and not using their intercession to obtain beauty, riches and such trifles. This, then, is how we receive the Holy Spirit through the mediation of the saints and of the Virgin.

Oh, how delightful and profitable it is to be visited by this holy Lady, for her visit always brings us many blessings. "O God," you will say, "I do wish the Virgin would visit me!" And why? "To be consoled, for it is so pleasant to have consolations! I would so love to have an ecstasy, a ravishment; indeed, I would very much like this sacred Virgin to show herself to me." Yes, and would you receive her as St. Elizabeth received her? Our Lady comes to visit us very often but we do not really want to receive her. Besides, St. Elizabeth was her relative, and that is why she went to seek her. But what can we do to become a relative of our amiable Sovereign? O God! There are a thousand ways of accomplishing this. Do you wish to be a relative of the Virgin? Communicate, for in receiving the Holy Sacrament, you receive the Flesh of her flesh and the Blood of her blood, since the precious Body of the Saviour, which is in the Divine Eucharist, was formed of her most pure blood by the operation of the Holy Spirit. Since it is impossible to be a relative of Our Lady in the same manner as Elizabeth, be so by imitating her virtues and her very holy life.

I shall finish with two examples; and although the time is up, nevertheless a short quarter of an hour will be justified. The first is about St. Gregory Thaumaturgus, the miracle-worker. Having been made bishop of a diocese in which there was very much work because of the heretics to be converted, he became subject to great fears and anxieties that he had not sufficient learning and eloquence to refute their errors. Then the holy Virgin appeared to him and instructed him, giving him full assurance of her continued assistance. She had with her her dear son of the Cross, namely, St. John the Evangelist, whom she commanded to write the profession of faith which she then gave to St. Gregory; he later inserted it in his *Opuscules,* where it can be seen to this day.

And here is another story: St. Gregory the Great relates it in his *Dialogues* as having happened in his time. I do not know if I have told it in this place; I do not have a good memory of it, but even though I may have already done so I will not fail to repeat it, because I am not in the presence of persons so particular that they cannot hear the same thing twice, for those with a good appetite enjoy the same dish a second time. But I must add this word also since it can be good and useful: There are some who are ready to banter and jest over the writings of this glorious saint, and indeed wrongfully, for St. Gregory was one of the greatest Popes that ever sat in the chair of Peter; a few years after his elevation to the papacy he withdrew into solitude and wrote the book of his *Dialogues.*

In it he relates that there was in the city of Rome a little girl aged seven, named Musa. This little Musette was greatly devoted to our sacred Mistress, and every day kissed her holy feet. Now one day Our Lady appeared to her, adorned as a Queen, beautifully robed, and accompanied by a multitude of young maidens all dressed in white. She addressed herself to little Musa and invited her to join these virgins—but she demurred, responding that she dared not do so. You see, she was very humble and polite. Our Lady went on to say: Ah now, my child, be very good and modest, but never coquettish. You will not live more than 30 days, for I will come to fetch you and take you away with these virgins.

Then she disappeared, and little Musa awoke to find herself completely changed; she took on an air of such great propriety and modesty that everyone was astonished, since this propriety surpassed her age. Her parents took her aside and asked the cause of the change; she replied that Our Lady had appeared to her with a troop of virgins and had told her not to be coquettish any more, but modest, because at the end of 30 days she would come to fetch her to take her away with her. Her father and mother did not pressure her because of the respect they bore the Holy Mother of God. At the end of 25 days the child was stricken with a prolonged fever which lasted five days, after which she died and Our Lady came to take her away.

Now we must draw a moral for ourselves from this story. Do you see, the Virgin visited little Musa, transformed and changed her totally. Transformation is the true mark of a divine visitation. We would indeed like to have revelations, but as a form of recreation, to pass the time, because they are indeed sweet and pleasing. Now, God does not give them for that; always they must cost us something. This visit cost the little Musa her life. Someone might have said to the Virgin: Ah, my Lady, how is it that you let this little girl suffer so much? She would have answered: Those who desire to share in my visits must always bring something of themselves.

We must then be firmly determined to suffer. And what? Dryness, aridity, disgust. It sometimes seems to us that we have been abandoned by God. You must endure all that if you wish to share in these visits, for to think that we can be devout without suffering is a delusion. Where there is more difficulty, there is more virtue.

Therefore, if you want the Virgin to visit you as she did the little Musa, there must be an interior transformation which cannot be effected without enduring something which is represented to us by the high fever this child suffered. Also, see if you have her confidence in Our Lady, for in order to be visited, confidence is necessary. In sum, we must humble ourselves as did St. Elizabeth, die to ourselves, and follow our divine Mistress in this life so that with her we can sing in her company on high: "My being proclaims the greatness of the Lord." [*Lk.* 1:46]. Amen, amen, amen.

NOTES

1. Cf. *Treatise*, Bk. 7, ch. 5.
2. Cf. Sermon for Mar. 25, 1621, p. 147; *Conferences*, VIII, p. 136.
3. Cf. Sermon for July 2, 1618, p. 50.
4. Cf. Sermon for Mar. 25, 1621, p. 147-148.
5. Cf. Sermon for July 2, 1618, p. 52-56.
6. Cf. Sermon for Mar. 25, 1621, p. 146; Sept. 10, 1620, p. 107; Aug. 15, 1618, p. 67.
7. Cf. Sermon for July 2, 1618, p. 50-51; Sept. 10, 1620, p. 106; Nov. 21, 1620, p. 121.
8. St. Francis was obviously negatively impressed with the superficiality, conceits, and courtly bearing of many men and women of nobility.
9. Cf. *Treatise*, Bk. 3, ch. 1.

— 12 —

THE PURIFICATION
OF THE BLESSED VIRGIN MARY

*Sermon for the Feast of the Purification, February
2, 1622, concerning the three names of this feast,
the Mystery of the Incarnation and the union of
the Divine and human natures in Our Lord, Our
Lady as the "new Eve," how Satan induced Eve to
hate God's commandment, our temptations to
hatred of God's commandments (which is the first
degree of disobedience), Our Lady's love for
God's commandments and for God who gave the
commandment, the "heresy" of choosing which
commandments we shall obey, and the happiness
of "carrying" Our Lord and of being "carried" by
Him.*

We celebrate today the Feast of the Purification of Our
Lady. Now this feast has three names. The Greeks and
Orientals call it the Presentation of the Son of God in the
Temple, because on this day Our Lady went up to
Jerusalem to present the only Son of God to His Eternal
Father in the very Temple of God. The second name is that
of the Purification of the Virgin, because the Law ordered
women to go to the Temple to be purified 40 days after
their delivery [*Lev.* 12:6-8] and to bring two animals for an
offering. (The pair of turtledoves offered by the sacred
Virgin [*Lk.* 2:24] was a sign and testimony of her Purification). Others call it the Feast of Meeting, because on this
day the different types of persons found in the Church of

172

God came together in the Temple. There we find Our Lady and St. Joseph, who were both virgins, yet married; St. Simeon who, according to the most common opinion of the ancient Fathers, was a priest; good Anna, a prophetess and a widow; and Our Lord, who is God and man. For this reason some call it the Feast of Meeting.[1] The third name given to the feast is that of St. Simeon the Just because he was in the Temple at that time, where he attained the fulfillment of his desires, and he witnessed to it by entoning his beautiful canticle, the *Nunc Dimittis.* [*Lk.* 2:29-32]. Now I thought it would be both profitable and agreeable to your hearts to say something to you on these three names.

As to the first, the Presentation of the Son of God in the Temple, I make this first consideration. Of all the sacrifices that had been offered to the Divine Majesty from the beginning of the world, none was equal to this in merit, inasmuch as the many holocausts and victims that had been immolated were vile and abject creatures such as sheep, goats, bulls or birds. [*Ps.* 40:7-8; *Heb.* 10:4-9]. But on this day the Son of God is offered to His Father in His own Temple. This offering is beautifully represented by the ceremonies we observe in the Church today, for the procession with lighted candles reminds us of that divine procession of the Virgin when she entered the Temple carrying in her arms her Son, who is the Light of the world. [*Jn.* 1:9; 8:12; 9:5]. Thus when Christians carry candles in their hands it is to testify that if it were possible they would carry Our Lord in their arms as did Our Lady and blessed Simeon, and would offer Him to the Eternal Father with as fervent a devotion as they now carry the candles that represent Him. This feast is the last of all those celebrated in honor of the Incarnation,[2] for from now on those which we shall celebrate in the liturgical cycle do not refer to this mystery or to the infancy of the Saviour, but rather to His Death, Resurrection and Ascension; in other words, they will be feasts of our Redemption. I shall then say a word about the Incarnation, since it concerns my subject.

This mystery is admirably represented by the candles which we carry today. A candle has one nature that is quite different from the separate natures of fire, wick and wax that are united to form it. Now in Our Lord also there are three substances which form only two natures, and these two natures, though distinct and remote from each other, form but one Person. These two natures are so closely united that the attributes and praises which are said of one are also said of the other; so that of this union it is equally true to say that God became man, and that man became God.[3] However, in the Incarnation God was made like unto us men [*Phil.* 2:7; *Heb.* 4:15] in human substance and nature, but not in [degree of] perfection, for in this He infinitely surpasses us.

The fire, which is the first and most excellent element in the candle, is a symbol of the Divinity. In a hundred places in Holy Scripture it is used to represent the Divine Nature, for there are many comparisons between fire and Divinity. I shall mention only a few. Fire is the first and principal of all created elements; Divinity is the source and supreme origin of all beings. Fire is subtile; Divinity has this property of subtility in a most noble and excellent degree. Fire has its dwelling in the third region of the air;[4] it always tends upward and throws its sparks higher, and remains upon earth only when united with some material substance. We do not see it as it is in its own proper sphere, because this [its own proper sphere] is the highest region of the air, from which it does not burn us, since its heat is tempered by the atmosphere. God dwells in Himself, His center being no other than Himself; hence when He determined to communicate Himself to man He went out of Himself as if by a divine effort and ravishment or ecstasy, in order to become united with His creation.[5] But He could not have dwelt on earth nor be seen by men [*Bar.* 3:38] if He had not taken to Himself a nature which would serve Him in some material way in order to retain Him. Fire always shoots out from its center, never knowing any repose. But God, who is

Himself His own proper center, neither comes nor goes. Yet He fills all things with His Divinity and finds His center everywhere because He is All in all. Fire is a light which enlightens; Divinity is a Light that lights up the darkness [*Jn.* 1:5; cf. *2 Pet.* 1:19], but Its brightness is so luminous and blinding that It is all darkness and obscurity so that It cannot be perceived nor apprehended in this life except by shadows and figures. [*Jn.* 1:18; *1 Tim.* 6:16]. Thus we see how the nature of fire represents the Divinity. I am not considering an infinity of other similarities between the two.

The other two elements of the candle, the wick and the wax, symbolize the soul and body of Our Lord. The wick united with the wax and fire gives an excellent light; but if we place it in the fire without being joined to the wax it will only send forth smoke or a very obscure flame. The nature of the wick is, without doubt, nobler than that of the wax. For wicks are ordinarily made of cotton, which grows very high on trees, while, on the contrary, everybody knows that wax is gathered like honey by bees from flowers which are near the ground. Truly the nature of the soul is far superior to that of the body; it is not corporeal nor earthly. And if it does not come from Heaven, still less does it come from earth; it is created by God at the same moment that it is infused into the body, which it embellishes and ennobles. In this life the soul without the body might, so to speak, still exist, but the manifestation of its feelings and emotions, its thoughts and sentiments, would be impossible without the senses, organs and members of the body. Man is therefore dual; for just as the body has need of the soul to give it vitality, so the soul, by a certain correspondence, requires this union with the body. In the same way, the wax, in order to give light, must be united with the wick—and the wick cannot do without the wax if it is to burn clearly. Now as we have said, the nature of the wax and that of the wick are different. One comes from the earth and is made by bees, while the other grows on big trees without any creature fashioning it, being made as it is by the Creator Himself. Nevertheless, these two natures are so united and mingled in the candles we carry that they make only a single candle, which fact is admirable.

The soul, as we have said, is entirely spiritual. It does not grow here below; it is created by God alone without the cooperation of any creature. But the body comes from the earth, for we know that the first man was formed out of the ground [*Gen.* 2:7] and, since that time, the body is formed from the substance of man and woman so that, for this reason, it is their work. Now although the soul and body are so different from one another, nevertheless they form one single person that we call man; they are so united by this union and joining that we speak of the two as if there were only one—just as when we speak of the excellence, the beauty, or other such qualities of a candle we do not make any distinction between the wick and the wax, but express it by only a single word: "This candle" is beautiful or good—speaking of the two natures found in it as if there were only one. The sacred body of Our Lord was not spiritual any more than that of other men, although it was more noble and excellent than ours, not having been conceived by the help of man, but by the Holy Spirit [*Mt.* 1:20; *Lk.* 1:35], who formed it of the most pure blood of the Virgin in such a way that this body is exactly like ours in substance. But His most holy soul was created by God, who at the very moment of its creation placed it in the body formed by the power of the Holy Spirit; and from thence these two substances of soul and body remained so joined and united that they formed but one perfect nature.

Fire, on being applied to the candle to light it, attaches itself more readily to the wick than to the wax, perhaps because its nature is more noble than that of wax and therefore more suited to be the first joined to the fire. In the Incarnation, the fire of Divinity, determining to unite Itself with human nature in order to render it all luminous, began by first attaching Itself to the wick—that is to say, to the soul of Our Lord. Now when I say that It was first united with His soul, represented by the wick, we must not understand this in such wise that, desiring to be enlightened on this Mystery of the Incarnation, we deceive ourselves. When I say that the Divinity attached Itself first to the soul of Our Lord, you must not imagine that this union between the Divinity and Jesus' soul took place two or three hours before the union with His sacred body. Oh no, for although the body of Our Lord was formed first, yet it did not exist one moment without being united with the soul. Likewise the soul and body of Our Lord did not exist one moment without being united to the Divinity. At the very moment that His soul and body were united in the womb of the Virgin, immediately the Divinity was united to both the one and the other. Nevertheless, this union began first with the soul as the more noble, and then passed to the body, but so subtly that both were united to the Divine Nature at the same time. This fact is well represented to us by the subtle way in which fire takes hold of the wick and the wax; for though it is first united with the wick, it is at the same instant united with the wax.

Now, this Divine Nature is so united and joined to the human nature and they form such a union and communion that man became God and God became man; moreover, the three substances were so united in the Person of Our Lord that they formed only two perfect natures, namely the human and the Divine, which, although infinitely removed from one another, nevertheless in the Incarnation form only one Person. This is all I have to say on the first name given to this feast.

The second name given to it is that of the Purification of the Virgin. Everyone is in unparalleled amazement to see this most holy Lady willing to subject herself to the law of purification, for she was a virgin and consequently had no need of it. Why then does she go to the Temple to be purified today? Indeed, until that time every woman who had become a mother was sullied as a consequence of Original Sin. That is why not only they, but also the children who were born of them, were in need of this cleansing, which they received in a very rigorous manner. Alas, even if we ourselves have not sinned, nevertheless we are all tainted with the guilt of our first father, Adam, and have made our entrance into the world under God's wrath [*Ps.* 51:7; *Eph.* 2:3], laden with the heavy weight of our iniquities. But this Divine Child had no more need of purification than His Mother, for not only was He not in sin, but what is more, He could not sin. It was impossible that sin should exist in Him—in Him, I say, who came to destroy it. He Himself proclaimed this. [*Jn.* 8:46; *Rom.* 8:3; *2 Cor.* 5:21]. "I am not," He could have said, "subject to the law of purification for I am the Son of God and therefore I have no sin in Me." This is an infallible truth.

Now as the Son was not sullied, neither was the Mother; for although it was not impossible for the Virgin to have had some sin, and being born of a mother and father she could have been slightly stained with it like other children, nevertheless it would not be fitting that the Mother of such a Son should be stained with Original Sin. This is the reason why, by a very special and singular privilege, this sacred Virgin, through divine grace, was conceived without sin;[6] she was most pure from her Conception and remained so in the Incarnation, for, having conceived by the overshadowing of the Holy Spirit [*Lk.* 1:35], she remained a virgin at childbirth and afterwards.

Why is it, then, that this most holy Lady, being all pure and without stain, wished to go to the Temple to be purified like other women—especially in view of the fact that this was not a universal law, but only a law established by Moses? There are thousands and thousands of reasons for it in the early Fathers, that is, with the ancient Doctors; but I shall make use of Genesis to show you why the sacred Virgin, although not obliged by the Law of Purification, chooses nevertheless to subject herself to it.

I shall then speak briefly about the fall of our first father and mother, Adam and Eve. [*Gen.* 2:15-17; 3:1-5]. This will not be out of place since Our Lord, of whom mention is made on this feast, is called the "new Adam" [*Rom.* 5:14; *1 Cor.* 15:45] who came to repair the sin of the first, and by His obedience make satisfaction for the other's disobedience; and Our Lady is called the "new Eve." [7] Now it is written that God created man and woman in original justice, which rendered them extremely beautiful and so capable of corresponding to grace that there was no sin at all in them, and consequently no struggle between the flesh and the spirit. [*Gen.* 1:27; cf. *Wis.* 2:23]. They had no repugnance to nor aversion for good, no desire nor inclination for evil; all in them was tranquil and peaceful; they enjoyed unparalleled happiness and peace; they lived in the greatest purity and innocence—not in a simple purity and innocence, but adorned with grace. The Lord placed them in this condition in Paradise and gave them but one commandment and prohibition: They were not to eat of the Tree of the Knowledge of Good and Bad; if they ate of it they would die.

Now Satan, that wicked spirit who had hurled himself down from Heaven by a disobedience proceeding from his self-love and self-esteem, envious of the beauty of human nature, planned to make it fall from this original justice which made it so beautiful and pleasing. Since self-love and self-esteem had caused his own disobedience, and, consequently, his damnation, he presented the same temptation to our first parents to see whether, with such a ruse, self-love and vain esteem would take hold on them as they had on him. This is why he took the form of a serpent, twined himself around a tree, and addressed himself first to Eve as to the weaker of the two, reasoning thus: "Why did God put you in this place and say you were not to eat from any of the trees that are here?" She answered him thus, surely frightened and trembling: "He has not forbidden us to eat of all the fruits, but only of this tree must we not eat, nor touch it."

A great temptation this—for it was a temptation to disobedience! Notice the malice and ruse of this infernal and
lying spirit. "Why," he asks, "did God say you were not to
eat of any of the trees?" Do you not see how he exaggerates God's prohibition? God had not forbidden them to eat
of any of the trees, but only of one; but the devil spoke
thus to Eve intending to make her hate the commandment
of the Lord; and this hatred is a great temptation against
obedience, for the first degree of disobedience is hatred of
the thing commanded. Lucifer, in his fall, began by a disgust for the commandment before his actual disobedience;
that is why, knowing the strength of this temptation,
although he knew that God had not forbidden our first
parents to eat of any of the trees, he did not hesitate to say
it to them in order to make them hate the command.

Please notice how this temptation increases with Eve's
reply: "We may eat indeed," she said, "the fruit of the
trees, except that of the Tree of Knowledge, which we must
not eat or touch. You ask me why? It is," she adds, "lest
perhaps we die." Notice the woman's great lie. True, God
had forbidden them to eat of the fruit of this tree, but not
to touch it or look at it—of this He had said nothing. It
was a lie as great as that of the evil spirit when he asked
why God had forbidden them to eat from any of these
trees. The aim of his temptation from the first was to get
Eve to make this reply, for by it she manifested disgust and
hatred, as if she had said: "He has not only forbidden us to
eat of it, but even to touch it and consequently to even look
at it—a very strange and severe thing." Behold disgust and
hatred for obedience, which is, as we have shown, the first
degree of disobedience.

We see also that all the wretched who are lost by withdrawing from the Church experience this disgust and
hatred for the commandments. For example, God has ordained that priests and ecclesiastics keep inviolate chastity
and virginity; but the devil comes to ask: "Why was this
commandment made?" And thus he succeeds in making

many hate it, and persuades them to withdraw from the Church that they may be freed from the obligation of observing it. Another will come to hate fasting or confession, and because of this hatred he also will go forth from the pale of Holy Church, and write against these precepts according to his passion. A great misfortune this, which happens only too frequently in these times of ours.[8]

I will give you a few examples to show you how great this temptation is. A father or a mother will forbid their daughter to go to a ball or a carnival or to associate with certain company. Hating this prohibition, she says: "I do not dare to think about a ball or carnivals. I do not dare to lift my eyes to look at a man; it would be better to have my eyes sewed up or plucked out or covered up like those of hawks."[9] Another professes to be a good Christian. He will say to himself: "It is Lent now and I must fast because it is a commandment of the Church; oh, I shall do so, but if I were Pope I should do away with Lent so that it would no longer be necessary to fast." And what is this but evidence of a dislike for the commandment? We observe it because it is of obligation, but we by no means like it, and if we could we would abolish it. A sister who does not like silence will say freely: "Oh dear! So much silence, what is the use of it? Would it not be better at this time to talk than to keep silence? Now that I have such an excellent thought it would do me so much good to tell it; it would give so much pleasure to those who heard it, and it is not permitted to tell it! Moreover, if I wait half an hour I will not remember it or know what it is." See how the dislike for silence makes her talk?

Another who does not like to go to the Office at the appointed times will be enjoying some good thought in her cell, and there it is: the bell that calls her to the Office. "Oh dear!" she will think, "wouldn't it be better not to go to Office? For in my cell I was enjoying such a beautiful thought; perhaps if I had remained a little longer I should have been rapt in ecstasy, and now I must go to the choir to sing." We ought to remain at table in silence until the end of the meal to hear the reading that is made there. "Oh dear, what is the use of all this? Would it not be better to go out when one has finished?" In short, it is a dislike of the commandments that makes us reason thus, and that makes us fail in obedience.

But the sacred Virgin voluntarily subjected herself to the law of purification because she loved the commandment, and the thing commanded was so precious to her. Although she was not obliged to it, she did not hesitate to fulfill it because of the love she had for obedience and for God who had given this commandment.[10] But, O most holy Lady, you have no need of it. "It is true," she replies; "but other women, for whom I should serve as an example, need it; I obey this law as much for the profit of those who are bound by it as because of the love I bear it."

Oh, how happy are those who love God's commandments and who keep not only those they are obliged to keep, but also those to which they are not bound, subjecting themselves for the good and edification of others. [Cf. *1 Cor.* 10:22-24]. It was this love that the sacred Virgin had for obedience and for the edification of the neighbor that made her submit to the law of purification.

The second temptation, or the second degree of the temptation to disobedience (I had intended to say three, but I will speak of only two), is the contempt not only for the commandment, but also for him who commands. Now when the temptation goes so far as to make us hate the one who commands, it is dangerous and extremely bad,[11] above all when it makes us say that he who commands has no reason for giving this command, that it is not to the purpose, and when it makes us utter words of contempt for the thing commanded or counseled because of the hatred we have for him who has commanded it.

I know indeed that we can have repugnances and aversions not only for the command, but also for those who command; but to comment or to entertain the thoughts suggested by these repugnances and aversions: This we should never do. However, it was at this that the evil spirit aimed, and for this reason he asked Eve, all the while despising the Lord's command: "Why did God give you this command?" He implies the question: "For what reason has He placed you in this paradise and forbidden you to eat of any of the trees that are here?" But he was a great liar, seeing that God had not given such a prohibition; and surely if He had done so it would seem to be intolerable, for to place a man and woman in a beautiful orchard full of fruit and command them not to touch a one of them would have been a very difficult command to observe.

Now, God did not enjoin this upon them; but the evil spirit said it in his contempt for God and with the intention of making Eve contemn Him. She in her turn did arrive at contempt for Him who gave them the command, and answered the tempter: "We may not eat of this fruit or, according to the words of the Lord, we may die." She said this by way of contempt for God. "He has threatened us," she would give him to understand, "with death if we eat of it; but what reason had He for such a threat against us?" Yet He did say: "lest you die." Do you see how these words of Eve manifest contempt? For God had not only said that they must beware of eating of this fruit for fear of death, but He had expressly declared that if they ate of it they would die. So much for the second degree of disobedience.

But our "new Eve," namely the sacred Virgin, loved, as we have already said, not only the commandment but Him who gave it. That is why she went up to Jerusalem to be purified, even though she was not subject to the law of purification. Without doubt she would have found more consolation in remaining in the poor cave of Bethlehem with her sacred Infant, continuing there the sweet and holy colloquies which took place between that Son and that Mother; but as she was truly obedient she showed no preference for one commandment more than for another, but submitted herself to them all indifferently—for true children of God do not choose which commands they will observe. It is the way of heretics to make such a choice: That is why they are called "heretics."[12]

But among Christians there must never be choice in what they are to believe and observe; they must simply believe. What must they believe? Everything, without exception. Nevertheless, we do find heresies of a sort among Christians—not indeed heresies of doctrine such as those of the heretics who are out of the Church, but heresies of disobedience committed by those Christians who wish to be good but who, despite that, are willing to obey only those commandments which please them.[13] You will see some who, in their love of fasting, would wish to fast even on Easter Sunday. Other such foolishnesses, no longer existing today, were seen in other ages. Some like the discipline, others the hair shirt; they want to do things which are counselled but not those that are commanded; they are willing to fast on Easter Sunday, which the Church does not command, but are unwilling to fast on Ash Wednesday! Oh no, we must not go to either extreme but must take the middle course, which is to obey without choice or preference.

There are other forms of the "heresy" in obedience: when we choose what we will observe; when we are unwilling to obey all kinds of commandments. It is this absolute and total obedience that places religious above even hermits and anchorites who lead a life in solitude that is more admirable than imitable. Is it not a wonderful thing to see St. Paul the Hermit dwelling in the midst of the desert, housed in a cave like a beast, his only nourishment bread and water? Yes, such things are admirable. Yet with all that, the saint had the use of his own liberty, a fact which lessened to some extent the austerities he performed, since in this manner of life he still exercised some choice and labored for his own particular salvation alone. I know well that he prayed for the whole world and that his prayers were very beneficial to humanity. Nevertheless it is an incontestable fact that religious perfection, that is to say, the manner of life of religious who are under obedience, far surpasses that of anchorites, for their obedience must be total and admit of no exception; they have no use of their liberty in the choice of their exercises, but rather submit themselves to the observance of their Rules and Constitutions and to the particular directions of their superiors. So much for the second name given to today's feast.

I must say a word on the third title given to this day, namely, the Feast of St. Simeon the Just. It is thus called because on this day that glorious saint received into his arms Him whom he had so longed for, but with joy and consolation so great that, having now nothing more to hope for and seeing his end near, he sang like a divine swan that beautiful canticle: Now, Master, You can dismiss Your servant in peace, for my eyes have witnessed Your saving deed.

To explain this third title I shall give you a very profitable example; and although I have alluded to it before in this place, I do not hesitate to offer it to you again inasmuch as many who are before me now were not present then. Besides, we do not, when speaking of the same subject, always say the same thing. The fact is this: Our Lord, seeing a little child one day, picked him up, kissed him and showed him to the Apostles, saying: I tell you solemnly, unless you become like this little child you will never enter Paradise. [*Mt.* 18:2-3; *Mk.* 9:35]. Many say that this child was St. Martial, who later became Bishop of Limoges; but the more common opinion is that it was St. Ignatius the martyr, whose feast we celebrated yesterday and whose Office is transferred to tomorrow. Oh, how blessed was this glorious St. Ignatius, since he was taken up into Our Lord's arms and given as an example to the Apostles! How precious and sweet was that kiss! What sacred, secret words Our Lord said to this happy child as He kissed him! How blessed he was to allow himself to be carried and handled by the Saviour, who rewarded him by engraving His own sacred Name in the depths of his heart!

Now tell me, please, whom do you consider to have been the happier: St. Ignatius, who was carried in Our Lord's arms, or St. Simeon the Just, who carried Our Lord in his arms? Tell me, which would you prefer: to be carried by this dear Saviour as was St. Ignatius, or to carry Him in your arms as did Simeon? Surely both were very happy— St. Ignatius in being handled and carried not where he willed but where it pleased Our Lord, and St. Simeon in carrying in his arms Him who produced such great happiness that he shed upon this Divine Saviour abundant tears of sweetness and consolation. But if you had to choose, which would you prefer? Think about it, for it will be a very useful reflection; and afterwards I will tell you my choice.

The great St. Ignatius was very happy in being carried in the arms of the Saviour and no longer walking with his own feet, but with those of Our Lord; for he who is carried walks not with his own feet but rather with the feet of him in whose arms he is carried. Oh, how happy is the soul who no longer journeys with his own feet, that is to say, according to his own thoughts and desires, nor according to his own preferences and inclinations! For the soul has spiritual feet as well as the body. How happy that soul when it no longer journeys according to its own desires, but rather according to those of its God. Now what are the desires of God but the commandments in which His will is expressed? And all are comprised in this first: You shall love the Lord your God with your whole heart, and your neighbor as yourself. [*Dt.* 6:5; *Mt.* 22:37-39]. From this come all the others: You shall not kill, you shall not steal [*Ex.* 20:13,15], and the rest which imply that you shall not do to your neighbor what you would not want done to yourself. There is no need then of putting ourselves to the trouble of trying to find out what are the desires of God, for they are all expressed in His commandments and in the counsels Our Lord Himself gave us in the Sermon on the Mount when He said: How blest are the poor in spirit, blest are the lowly, and the other beatitudes. [*Matt.* 5:3-10]. These are all the desires of God upon which we ought to walk, following not only His precepts but also His counsels and intentions as perfectly as we can.[14] This is what we do when we obey the general inspirations which are indicated in the Rules and Constitutions, as well as the particular and secret ones which He places in the depths of our hearts. But to walk securely according to the divine desires, we must be simple and sincere in our efforts to discover them, and we must follow the direction given us about them. By this means we shall be carried by Our Lord and shall walk no more according to our own desires, but according to those of God.

The glorious St. Simeon also was very happy to carry the Saviour in his arms. I will suggest two ways in which we carry Him and then I will conclude. The first is to bear Him upon our shoulders as did St. Christopher; the second is to hold Him in our arms as did St. Simeon and Our Lady. Surely, although St. Christopher carried Our Lord only on his shoulders, yet he was highly favored, and merited to be called the Christ-bearer. Now, to carry Him in this way is nothing else than willingly to endure and suffer with a good heart all that it pleases Him to send us, however difficult and heavy be the charge and burden that God places upon our shoulders. How can His yoke be easy [*Mt.* 11:30] if we imagine ourselves exempt from suffering? No, we must—like St. Christopher—carry Our Lord on our shoulders, enduring all that He pleases, in the way He pleases, and for as long as He pleases, abandoning ourselves entirely to His eternal Providence, allowing ourselves to be governed and led according to His holy will.

The second way is to carry Him as did Our Lady and St. Simeon. We do this when we endure with love the labors and pains He sends us, that is to say, when the love which we bear to the Law of God makes us find His yoke easy and pleasing, so that we love these pains and labors, and gather sweetness in the midst of bitterness. This is nothing else but to carry Our Lord in our arms. Now if we carry Him in this way, He will, without doubt, Himself carry us. Oh, how happy we shall be if we allow ourselves to be carried by this dear Lord, and if we carry Him on our shoulders as did St. Christopher and in our arms as did St. Simeon, abandoning ourselves entirely to Him and letting Him lead us where He pleases! Leave yourselves, then, entirely in the arms of His Divine Providence, submitting yourselves in what concerns His Law and disposing yourselves to endure all the pains and suffering that may come to you in this life. When you have done this you will find that the hardest and most painful things will be rendered sweet and agreeable to you, and you will share the happiness experienced by St. Simeon and St. Ignatius. But as to which of these was the happier, that is not for me to say; I leave that to you to think upon and decide for yourselves. Only try to imitate them in this life and you will bless the Saviour and be blessed by Him in Heaven, together with these glorious saints. In the name of the Father, and of the Son, and of the Holy Spirit. Amen.

NOTES

1. St. Francis de Sales considers the Feast of Meeting as a variation on the second name, the Purification of the Virgin.
2. The Feast of the Purification traditionally ends the Christmas season.
3. Cf. Sermon for July 2, 1621, p. 156.
4. St. Francis is following here the cosmology of Aristotle.
5. Cf. *Treatise,* Bk. 10, ch. 17.
6. Cf. Sermon for Feb. 2, 1620, p. 86.
7. Cf. Sermon for July 2, 1621, p. 162.
8. St. Francis is alluding, of course, to the Reformation and to the challenges made to priestly celibacy, religious life and many of the Sacraments and precepts of the Roman Catholic Church.
9. Cf. *Conferences,* XII, "On Simplicity," p. 221, note 6.

10. Cf. *Conferences,* XIII, "On the Spirit of the Rules," p. 251-252; Sermon for Nov. 21, 1620, p. 131-132.
11. Cf. *Conferences,* I, "Obligation of the Constitutions," p. 2-3.
12. St. Francis de Sales is alluding here to the root meaning of the word "heretic," which is "to choose."
13. Cf. *Treatise,* Bk. 10, ch. 9.
14. Cf. *Treatise,* Bk. 9, ch. 4; *Conferences,* V, "On Generosity," p. 83.

THE IMMACULATE CONCEPTION
OF THE BLESSED VIRGIN MARY

Sermon for the Feast of the Immaculate Concep-
tion, December 8, 1622, concerning feasts, the es-
sence of our Faith, Lucifer's sin, the fall of Adam
and Original Sin, the transmission of Original Sin,
miracles performed for Jeremiah and St. John the
Baptist, the Immaculate Conception of Our Lady,
and what Our Lady truly desires of us.

The shortness of time and leisure which the turmoil of
the world leaves us is the reason why I shall talk to you
very simply and familiarly (for it seems to me that in these
matters it is better so) on the two points which I was not
able to explain last Thursday, that is to say, how we should
celebrate feasts and what are the feasts and mysteries
which we celebrate. I have always been accustomed to announce the subject before speaking of it.

In the first place, we should know that there are three
kinds of feasts: those which the Church commands us to
celebrate, those which she recommends,[1] and political
feasts, an example of which is celebrated today for the en-
try of the king into this city. Since it is ordained by the of-
ficials of the city, it is thus political.

The feasts are recommended to us in order to render to
God the honor, the cult, and the adoration which we owe
Him as our Sovereign Master and Lord. The Feast of the
Conception of the Virgin is not commanded us, but is
strongly recommended.[2] To invite us to the devotion and

solemnity of this feast, the Church, as a charitable Mother, grants us indulgences, and with this intention she does the same for confraternities. St. Jerome and St. Bernard recommend it to us in the breviary and the homilies of this day.

But first, before entering more fully into our discourse, let me say this word for the instruction of Christians on the essence of our Faith. We must know, first of all, that there are four parts to it: The first is what we should believe, the second what we should hope for, the third what we should love, and the fourth what we should do and practice.

The first is included in the Apostles' Creed, which is so called because it was composed by the Apostles. In it is contained all that we are obliged to believe—if not in detail, at least in general. For example, it is not said in the Creed that there are angels. Nevertheless, it is a truth which we believe and find in Holy Scripture—and even that they are employed in ministries here below in this world. Heretics want to insist that the Holy Sacrifice of the Mass is not included in our Creed. These unfortunate people have advanced this theory to see if anyone would be so weak-minded as to believe their errors. But, my dear souls, I tell you there are a hundred articles in our Faith which are not explicitly expressed in our Creed, which nevertheless all Christians ought to believe. They should not say: "I am content to believe what the Church believes," and so remain in that unpardonable ignorance.

All that we ought to hope for and ask of God is contained in the seven petitions of the Our Father, which we commonly call The Lord's Prayer and which Our Lord left us. [*Matt.* 6:9-13].

For the third we have the divine commandments by which we are instructed to love God and our neighbor, for on these two commandments the whole Law is based, and the prophets as well. [*Matt.* 22:37-40]. You know also those which follow, that is, the Ten Commandments and the precepts of the Church. The Church resembles a beautiful tree, or better, the orange tree which is always

green—in all seasons. Indeed, in Italy on the coast of
Genoa, and still more in this country of France—as, for example, in Provence—all along the waterfront the trees bear
leaves, flowers and fruits at every season. (Assuredly, the
orange tree is always in the same state, never withering,
even when it is not nourished.) Thus the Church has her
foliage, which are her ceremonies; her flowers, which are
her actions; and her fruits, which are her good works and
the good example which she gives to her neighbor on all
occasions.

Further, there are the seven Sacraments. We are not, of
course, obliged to receive them all, but only each according
to his or her vocation. For example, the Sacrament of Holy
Orders is for priests, and that of Matrimony is for those
whom God calls to it. As for the others, we must use them
according to time and place and receive them according as
the Church commands us, for we are bound to this.

Let us come to our second point, namely, what feasts we
are to celebrate. Let us consider first of all that God,
despite being a pure and free spirit, willed to create something outside Himself and thus created the angels, and
afterwards Adam and Eve in the state of innocence and
original justice. Furthermore, He left them their free will,
accompanied by all the prerogatives and privileges of grace
which they could possibly desire. But what did Lucifer do,
that spirit of revolt, when he saw himself endowed with so
excellent a nature? He did not wish to subject himself in
any way whatever.

Now, you know that all the angels were created in grace
but were not confirmed in grace at once; God left them
their free will and full liberty. When this first angel,
Lucifer, saw that he was so beautiful and so excellent in
his nature—for he was the most perfect of all—he said to
himself: I will take my seat in the recesses of the North,
which are the highest; I will be like the Most High! [*Is.*
14:13-14]. All will render me honor. When St. Michael saw
that, he cried out: Who is like God! [Cf. *Is.* 40:18] and by

this means he threw Lucifer into the recesses of the pit [*Is.* 14:11-15; *Rev.* 12:7-9], according to the writings of St. Bernard, for no one can be elevated unless he has first humbled himself. [Cf. *Matt.* 18:14, 23:12; *Lk.* 14:11, 18:14].

Thus Lucifer became a rebel against his Creator and therefore against the image of his Creator, who is man. He addressed himself to our first parents and primarily to Eve, speaking to her in this way: If you eat of this fruit, you will know good and evil and will be like God. She listened willingly to this suggestion (for as soon as someone speaks of exalting us in some way, it seems that our whole being depends upon it); she gave her consent and ate the forbidden fruit. Even going further, she gave some to her husband to eat, both thus succumbing and becoming disobedient to God. At that very instant they became ashamed and confused, for sin brings such with it, and they hid themselves from God as far as it was possible for them. [*Gen.* 3:1-11].

If they had remained in grace, we would have participated in that incomparable good, for it is from their fall that Original Sin has taken its source. It is the heritage which they left us, just as we might have had the same inheritance of that grace and justice in which they had been created, had they persevered. But alas, they remained in it for only a short while—it was only a moment; and since we are all of the same stock and seed as Adam, we are all tainted with Original Sin. This is what made the great royal prophet cry out: In guilt was I born, and in sin my mother conceived me. [*Ps.* 51:7]. This means that we are all conceived in sin, and all conceptions from the beginning of the world to the end will be made in sin.

It is true indeed that our first father, and Eve too, were created and not conceived. Nevertheless, every human conception is made in sin. Our Lady and holy Mistress alone was exempt from this evil—she who was to conceive God first in her heart and in her spirit before conceiving Him in

her chaste womb. All are born under God's wrath [*Ps.*
51:7; *Eph.* 2:3] because of Original Sin, which makes them
enemies of God. But by Baptism they are regenerated and
become His children, capable of His grace and of the
heritage of eternal life. All have been stained with Original
Sin, but some have been purified before their birth by a
special miracle, as was St. John the Baptist and also the
prophet Jeremiah. [*Jer.* 1:5]. At the words of the sacred
Virgin Mary, St. John was sanctified by the presence of
Him who was enclosed in her womb. Our Lord and St.
John the Baptist visited each other in the wombs of their
mothers (the wombs of our mothers are little worlds), and
it is said that the glorious Precursor placed himself on his
knees in adoration of his Saviour and that at the same instant he was given the use of reason.[3] But the world will
believe only what it sees. (Be this said in passing.)

However, St. John and Jeremiah were conceived in sin
by the ordinary way of generation. This was not so with
Our Lord, who was conceived of the Holy Spirit and of His
sacred Mother [*Matt.* 1:18, 20; *Lk.* 1:35], without any
father. This is why He could not reasonably inherit Original Sin. You may say: Since He has taken our nature, He is
human. That is true, but He is also God, and because of
this He is perfectly God and man without any separation or
distinction whatsoever. He is not of Adam's seed through
generation because He was conceived of His Mother without a father, as we have just said. He was of the stock of
Adam, to be sure, but not of the seed [of Adam].

As for Our Lady, the most holy Virgin, she was conceived in the usual way of generation. But since in His plan
God had predestined her from all eternity to be His
Mother, He kept her pure and free from all stain, although
by her nature she could have sinned. There is no doubt
about that, as far as actual sin is concerned.

Let me make a comparison in order that you may understand better. Do you know how pearls are made? (Many
ladies desire pearls but they do not care about their origin.)

Mother-of-pearl fish do as the bees do. They have a king and choose for that role the largest among them, the rest following him. They come on ocean waves when the air is freshest, which is at break of day, principally in the month of May. When they are all there they open their shells toward Heaven, allowing drops of dew to fall into them. They then clamp shut upon these drops in such a manner that they incubate this dew drop and convert it into a pearl, which is then considered so valuable. But notice, they close their shells in such a way that no salt water enters.[4]

This comparison will serve my purpose well. The Lord has done the same for the Blessed Virgin, Our Lady, because at the instant of her Conception He placed Himself between her and sin—or rather, one might say, *under* her, to prevent her from falling into Original Sin. In the above example, if the drop of dew does not find the shell to receive it, it will fall into the ocean and be converted into briny and salty water. But if the shell receives it, it is changed into a pearl. In the same way the most holy Virgin was cast into the sea of this world by the common way of generation, but preserved from the salty water of the corruption of sin. It was fitting that she have this particular privilege because it was not reasonable that the devil be able to reproach Our Lord with the claim that she who had carried Him in her womb had [in Original Sin] been subject to him. It is for this reason that the Evangelist does not make mention of the father and mother of the Virgin, but only of Joseph, the husband of a Virgin named Mary. It was of her that Jesus who is called the Messiah was born.[5] [*Matt.* 1:16]. Thus by a special grace her soul possessed nothing [of Original Sin] from her earthly parents, as is the case with all other creatures.

Let me now say something of the devotion which we ought to have toward this holy Virgin. The worldly-minded imagine that devotion to Our Lady usually consists in carrying a rosary in their cincture. It seems to them that it is enough to pray it a number of times without doing anything else. In this they are greatly mistaken. For our dear Mistress wants us to do what her Son commands us [*Jn.* 2:5] and considers as done to herself the honor we give to her Son by keeping His commandments.

We have some examples of this. I shall content myself with citing one or two. When the mother of the Emperor Nero, that cruel monster who so persecuted the Church of God, was pregnant, she made the enchanters and soothsayers come in order to find out what her child would become. When they were being consulted, one of them announced that this child would be emperor, that he would reign and be great. However, another, perceiving that the first flattered her, told her that the child would indeed be emperor, but as emperor he would put her to death. Then this miserable mother replied: It does not matter "provided he reigns."[6] Notice how the vainglorious desire honors and pleasures which oftentimes are prejudicial to them. We have another example in the Third Book of Kings, chapter one,[7] where it is said that when Queen Bathsheba went to David, she offered him many acts of homage. [*1 Kgs.* 1:16-17]. In seeing that, the king well knew that she required something and asked her what it was. Bathsheba answered: "Sire, that my son might reign after you." Now, if mothers are naturally so desirous that their children might reign and be honored, with much greater reason is Our Lady, who knows that her Son is her God. Thus the honor of the Son is also that of the Mother.[8]

But for our consolation let me say this word. You, my very dear Sisters, who have left the world to place yourselves under the patronage of the most holy Virgin,[9] if you question her and say: "Mother, what can we do to please you?" no doubt she will answer that she desires and wants you to do what she directed to be done at that celebrated marriage feast of Cana in Galilee when the wine gave out. She said to those who had the care of it: Do whatever my Son tells you. [*Jn.* 2:5]. If then you listen to her faithfully, you will hear in your heart those very words addressed to you: Do whatever my Son tells you. May God give us the grace to listen to her in this life and in the other. Amen.

NOTES

1. Cf. Volume 1 of this series, *The Sermons of St. Francis de Sales on Prayer,* p. 17.
2. The Feast of the Immaculate Conception was not a holy day of obligation in France at this time.
3. Cf. Sermon for July 2, 1621, p. 161.
4. Cf. *Introduction,* Author's Preface.
5. Apparently St. Francis de Sales finds support for Mary's Immaculate Conception in the fact that her parents are not mentioned by the Evangelist.
6. Cf. *Treatise,* Bk. 10, ch. 8.
7. In newer editions of the Bible, this text is found in the First Book of Kings.
8. Cf. Sermon for August 15, 1602, p. 22-23.
9. St. Francis is speaking to the Sisters of the Visitation of Holy Mary.

INDEX
Index to the Sermons

198

Index to the Scriptural References